Advanced Praise for

"The proposal for a life without the obsession with winning makes sense in a society as competitive as ours. To really reach a full state of well-being, we need to recognize our thoughts, feelings and actions, and the book proposes exactly this path of reflection. It is a complete book, with theory added to practice, which guides us without caring, induces without determining. Note the research and years of accumulated knowledge of its authors. It has the necessary density for decision-making and the tranquility of possible trajectory proportions."

--Marta Gucciardi, Brazil

"I found this book really inspiring and relevant given the recent life changes during the pandemic. It's very thorough and easy to read in order to implement the exercises to change your life. Highly recommend this book for anyone who is looking to transcend to the next level of their life!"

--Richard Gomez, Spain

"The Exponential Individual Playbook' is an important resource for anyone seeking to live a meaningful life while doing their best work in the world. The authors are the living proof of this, having collaborated as a small team to produce this book. Bravo to them! And well done to the reader who, page by page, will learn how to take their human potential to new heights."

--Sophie Krantz, Australia

"Freedom from social conditioning to discover your true self and purpose is masterfully orchestrated in this book. Through unearthing layers upon layers of wisdom from the sages of the ages, skillfully reinterpreted, you experience transcendent meaning and transformation. This is much more than a self-help book on how to become an exponential game changer to better yourself and the world you are an integral part of. You will breeze through the reading, occasionally resting to smell the fragrances and contemplate your existence, consciousness, and bliss, and often, set your imagination free to live your best life, transform the human spirit, and better the world."

--Stephen Earnhart, Switzerland

"Exponential dynamics are not only outside of you but inside you as a human being. The attributes such as awareness, compassion, attention, fulfillment or attention and curiosity or responsibility… are exponential potentials in itself that we have at no costs! It is there by design and we only need to cultivate them. That's exactly what this playbook is about."

--Paul Epping, the Netherlands

The Exponential Individual Playbook

*Live Your Best Life, Transform the Human Spirit
and Better the World*

CO-AUTHORED BY THE PEOPLE BEHIND EXI

Kindle Direct Publishing
P.O. Box 8075
Grand Rapids, MI 49518
United States

Cover Design: Philip Earnhart

First Edition April 27, 2023
Printed in the United States of America

ASIN BOBZ13SG78 (Kindle eBook)
ISBN 979-8-9882613-9-1 (hardcover)
ISBN 979-8-9882613-6-0 (paperback)

To all the contributors of this initiative thus far, words can not express how much we appreciate you and all of your efforts. The launch of the ExI playbook is just the beginning of a beautiful and challenging ride ahead, but without a doubt…Together. We. Can!

– Ann Boothello & Eric Patel

To Eric, a dear and special member of my soul tribe, and co-founder of the ExI initiative. I'm forever grateful for our friendship and your unwavering belief in our ability to serve humanity despite the struggles we may face in our own personal lives. The faith you have in me, the team and yourself to push forward is testament to your strength in character and the values you live by, some of these being courage, perseverance, kindness and love. The ExI playbook is one of the many ways our work will inspire people to look within to heal and lead more authentically. Thank you for being on my journey.

– Ann Boothello

To Ann, my multi-talented business partner and co-founder, very dear friend and lifelong soul connection, I wouldn't have wanted to birth and grow ExI with anyone but you. This passion project has been a labor of love for us for the past year and a half and I'm forever grateful for all of your energy, efforts, faith and light. I know that together by leveraging this playbook we'll reach even more people to optimize their personal transformation along their lifelong journey in service to humanity. Thank you for believing in me, standing by my side, having my back and co-piloting this amazing adventure we're on together.

– Eric Patel

Contents

Foreword

The need for individuals to take charge of their well-being is increasingly important given the global, regional and personal challenges we face. The Exponential Individual Playbook is a unique resource that enables people to deepen their self-awareness and accelerate their human transformation. It lays out a flow of stages of personal transformation and showcases various best practice tools and techniques that you can test to create a more meaningful, fulfilled life.

This important book is not meant to be read from start to finish but rather to inspire you wherever you are on your personal journey. It is not meant to be prescriptive but rather suggestive and collaborative, offering pathways for you to look within and become the change you want to see in the world.

The ExI Playbook emphasizes the importance of both the brain and the heart in personal transformation. Productivity, performance, output, results and 5-10x growth are important, but so are consciousness, self-awareness, intention and intuition. We all have limited time and it's important that you make your life, experiences and impact meaningful, heartfelt and enduring.

Exponential Individuals were formed to make self-awareness, human optimization and collective betterment universal. The ExI co-creators are playing at the intersection of consciousness and technology to birth a wellbeing model that inspires a new way of being.

The Exponential Organizations book I wrote addressed how companies can attain massive impact and results by leveraging exponential technologies and new organization techniques. The Exponential Individual Playbook addresses the individual person and the journey that is needed to make not only organizations transform exponentially but all of the groups that individuals exist within. This is critical to the evolution of humanity and thus, the planet.

The future holds extraordinary potential for exciting developments at this intersection.

Salim Ismail
Founder, OpenExO
Tenafly, New Jersey, USA
March 20, 2023

Prologue

Contributor: Howard Rankin

Have you heard the song *Vivere*, written by singer-composer Gerardino Trovata and performed by Andrea Bocelli? It translates as "Dare to Live," and encourages listeners to do just that: escape societal conventions, old habits and self-limiting notions to become the best version of themselves.

We all need to dare to live a meaningful life. And it's a lifelong process.

Many young people in their late teens and early twenties today are struggling. We have a friend whose son is a smart young man but troubled by the fact that at 20 he still doesn't know "what he wants to do." Why should he be at his age?

In the boomer generation, society was more rigid and less dynamic. If you were smart and lucky, you went to college and embarked on your lifetime career. You got a job and stayed in it until you retired. Today, however, change is so dynamic that the job you enter in your early twenties will certainly change dramatically - and might not even exist within a decade, let alone a few years.

This fast-changing world has implications for every generation. Retirement today is not what it was fifty years ago. Many retirees today have the prospect of a good twenty years or more of being productive in different ways. In fact, the word "retirement" is outdated. Why define a critical period of life by something you no longer do: go to a job every day?

As far as the younger generations go, adolescence ends at 35. Not physical growth, but by your mid-thirties you should have a decent understanding of who you are, what makes you tick and what is important to you. Not that you can't dare to live before then; of course, you can. However, you need experience that is critical in shaping your sense of yourself, and tools and guidance of how to identify and develop your skills. That's what this book is about.

Career advice typically is about the qualifications and attributes needed for particular professions. While this book touches on some of that, it's not so much a playbook for those in a particular profession but a playbook for those who dare to live. It's a playbook for everyone: teens, young adults and older adults.

Vivere![1]

It's never too late to manifest your latent talents and skills. It's never too late to find meaning. It's never too late to find new meaning. It's never too late to make a difference. It's never too late to dare to live. And daring to live requires some serious self-examination.

---

[1] You can see a video of this song being sung by Bocelli and Trovata in this video. They start singing around the 1:20 mark. You can find the Italian and English lyrics here: The English lyrics are also in the last chapter of this playbook.

Self-help…we all need it, don't we? Yet how many of us help *ourselves*?

Suffice to say that there are many titles that have been written over the years in the self-help / personal development / personal success / self-improvement category.

The co-authors to The Exponential Individuals Playbook acknowledged this and decided instead of making another contribution to this overcrowded field, we would co-create something that suggests phases of one's transformation and would remain open to evolve its content over time with community. We are not claiming that the contents of this book are unique; we are offering starting points depending on where our readers are along their journeys. This would allow nearly anyone to make self-awareness and human optimization not an exception but the rule. The playbook is one component of many that the team at Exponential Individuals (ExI) are co-creating to support our collective evolution.

We asked ourselves how could human beings access and manage the unlimited potential that is already in themselves? Could this be harnessed? Could it be sustained? And what techniques and resources are available?

Inspired by the book *Exponential Organizations* and how companies can access and manage abundance that is present in the world, ExI was born in the midst of the COVID-19 pandemic in March 2021 to help others find their quest for meaning and their journey in life. It certainly didn't take a worldwide pandemic for humanity to realize that several forces were already in motion including but not limited to:

- Systems collapsing worldwide.
- Organized religion dismantling.
- People challenging history, traditions, science, and the status quo.
- Humanity is looking for a deeper sense of meaning.

Spoiler alert: you already are a person with massive potential. Reading this book and applying the practices that you are drawn to will inspire you on a path towards becoming an Exponential Individual. You just need to tap into what you already have that's lying dormant within. This playbook will show you how by exploring multiple pathways for you to be at your best, moment by moment.

This book includes many of the strategies and tools that have been advanced over the years to inspire and help people manifest real change in their lives. This combination of the foundational wisdom contained in the exponential movement as highlighted in the book *The School of Life: An Emotional Education*, and proven and researched strategies for behavioral, neurological and spiritual change, we hope provides you with all you need to understand and manifest a new way of being. Vivere!

References

Alain de Botton. (2020). *The School of Life: An Emotional Education.*

Salim Ismail (Author), Michael S. Malone (Author), Yuri van Geest (Author), Peter H. Diamandis (Foreword) (2014)

Exponential Organizations: Why New Organizations Are Ten Times Better, Faster, and Cheaper Than Yours (And What To Do About It). Diversion Books.

Chapter 1

The Increasing Need for Exponential Individuals

"The greatest shortcoming of the human race is our inability to understand the exponential function."

— Albert A. Bartlett

Contributors: Ann Boothello, Eric Patel, Howard Rankin

Definition of Exponential

Exponential: rising or expanding at a steady, rapid rate; any positive constant raised to a power.

In his book *Recapture the Rapture*, James Wheal highlights the fact that human beings have hardly evolved and that we basically are "primates wearing clothes." In an exponentially changing world this has led to a major crisis with increasing undigested trauma and disconnection from meaning and each other. One of his core ideas on creating a sense of meaning in our lives was based on the work done by The Sacred Design Lab at Harvard Divinity School. They summarized that faith has three components: Beyond, Becoming, and Belonging - the vital ingredients for a human to thrive. Or also expressed as **inspiration**, **healing**, and **connection**. This isn't new, the ancient Greeks called them *ecstasis, catharsis,* and *communitas.*

However, did we somehow lose the plot? Numerous factors have led to this situation in which many people find themselves disconnected and leading lives that lack meaning or purpose.

Can we honor our human needs for healing, connection, and inspiration and offer solutions that are open source to encourage that, available to everyone and "antifragile," i.e., resilient and adaptive?

The Productivity Obsession

For decades we've been focused on a way of defining time well-spent in a manner that has distanced us from a life of deeper meaning and purpose. That focus has been productivity, worse yet, uninspired, unaligned productivity: a way of being that translates into purposeless 'productivity' and moving further away from personal meaning.

The "need" to be productive often stems from a need to be validated by society or to validate oneself as "useful." This is like driving a car aimlessly until it runs out of fuel and leaves you wondering why you bothered. Now imagine another scenario where you feel like going for a drive because you have to pick up groceries or you're seeking novelty and want to drive down a new road to discover where it leads. In these scenarios a person knows why they want to do what they want to do which is to drive the car. What we're suggesting is that productivity in its traditional context is lacking individual purpose. The old way of viewing productivity applied well for factories and machines because the effort that we put in was directly proportional to the results that came out.

However, for an individual the factors at play are contrastingly different.

Productivity encapsulates the universal law of cause and effect and has been traditionally measured without acknowledgement of (1) the individual psyche's need for rest, emotional and physical healing, integration and restoration; nor (2) the individual's drive to make an effort in life that can stem from a variety of things from a lack of energy due to poor nutrition and fitness, to a lack of purpose or a will to live.

In many work environments today, a well-rested person working for 8 hours a day who gets great results is more valuable than someone who works 12-hour days and gets burned out. Yet most of us continue to measure and reward results rather than efforts, product rather than purpose.

Child psychology suggests it can be harmful to focus on results rather than effort for creating well-rounded individuals. In a recent study in the *Journal of Experimental Psychology* James et al., state that parental criticism is associated with many detrimental child outcomes and that:

"These findings suggest that children exposed to maternal criticism may exhibit disruptions in adaptive responses to environmental experiences."

For instance, if a parent praises a grade A as opposed to a C+ for effort, the child may lose enthusiasm and not feel good enough. On the other hand, if one praises effort and says, "Look at that, you did well, you can achieve so much more if you want to. That's exciting!" This encourages a child to strive for more while believing s/he is good enough.

The Hard Truth

Let's take a look at some of the more disturbing facts. Some of you might have seen the Harvard Business Review Study called *Beyond Burned Out*. The most interesting aspect of this is how much of the study was completed pre-pandemic and how normalized this self-critical state has become across all work cultures. If you are struggling to get through the day, if you are constantly interrupted, if you always feel you are dropping the ball and if you cannot switch off at the end of the day, you are now the normal one. This current dysfunction of our society is clearly unsustainable. We are in the middle of a mental health crisis and yet we are asking people to be more flexible and adaptable for the sake of a bottom line to which they often feel almost entirely disconnected.

The Role Technology Has Played In Getting Us To This State

We believe it's a mistake to think of this as a COVID-related problem. Sure, COVID has shined a light on and amplified the problem but it has been a long time coming and technology has played an enormous enabling role. For the past 30 years, wave after wave of technology innovations have come. There are many that appear small on the surface; however, each of these waves has compounded into an enormous effect: disruptive, exponential technologies such as artificial intelligence (AI), nanotech, blockchain and cryptocurrencies. The takeaway here is what is driving these innovations: a desire for flexibility and the ability to do anything, anywhere, at any time. And it has been largely effective. All of us can now be reached anywhere at any time: we have apps on our mobile devices to do real work whether we are on a video call from a home office in Boston, messaging from our friend's home in Dubai or speaking at a conference in Barcelona.

In our always-on culture this inevitably leads to stress, burnout, mental health issues or worse. It also leads to a definition of ourselves that is centered almost exclusively around our occupation or our addiction to remain occupied with anything to feel useful. Coupled with living in the attention economy (it is estimated that some of us are exposed to as many as 10,000 ads a day) with constant information overload, this is a recipe for a disaster in the making.

So how did we get here and what does it mean for the future of work, workers and life in general?

The changes come down to human imagination to design technology that gives us globally increased productivity and flexibility. There have been dozens of technology innovations that have sent us down this path but the categories of focus can be largely divided into two overlapping groups.

The first group is probably best called "personal productivity'" which started in the 1980s with personal computing and really took off in the 1990s. As personal computers (PCs) began to arrive on our desks it became clear that not only could technology improve overall productivity but it could also make humans themselves more productive in the workplace. Today, software helps all of us do more in less time just as our dishwashers and washing machines help us get the housework done in a fraction of the time as compared to our ancestors. If you are using a computer to help you do your job today it's probably saving you hours each day when compared to paper-based alternatives. Think of sending emails or texts versus letters, knocking out a presentation in PowerPoint versus transparencies or creating a financial model in Excel instead of using a ledger.

The second group can be considered "flexible workstyle." These changes began around the same time but achieved something very different and sometimes even reduced our personal productivity. These innovations which include multitasking operating systems, the web, the extranet, mobility and app stores, have combined to allow us to work with anyone, at any time, in any place and in almost any way.

If the first group makes us more efficient at doing work, the second makes it more effective for us to do work in the first place and therefore makes it harder to break from it.

People Are Not Properly Prepared For The New Reality

Things are very different nowadays. For many of us there is no defined start or end to our workday. We might be doing any type of activity at any time, switching contexts constantly, with no breaks. And those people we work alongside? They are quite often on a completely different schedule than us. Somehow we have to figure out how to be effective as individuals and teams scattered across the globe. It's a real wonder we ever get anything done.

Many people assume that this is a set of underlying skills we should all have naturally like the way all able-bodied people can run. But just like running, there is a better way to run and the common way most of us run. These two things are very different. Why should we expect to have these skills well-honed in the first place?

Work and its relationship with our broader lives have changed so dramatically and quickly that the skills we need to thrive in it have just not had time to develop, similar to how our brains have not adapted to a changing world. And the rate of change in our workplaces is not going to slow down. People have discovered ways to adapt their work lives around their personal lives (instead of the other way around) including time to sleep, rest and have fun (yes that's important too!). And if you've put in the time to discover you, well, your work too, can also be fun.

What Has Changed?

If you were in the workplace 30 - 40 years ago chances are you got a lot more rest and sleep. If you were like most workers your day started at around 9am and when you shut the door on it physically at 5pm you shut the door on it mentally as well. This amounted to 16 hours of non-work every single workday plus a 64-hour break every weekend. That's a full and complete break from every work system, work conversation and piece of digital technology (aside from perhaps a TV screen).

People are also living longer. In 1970 the average lifespan was 77 years for women and 72 years for men. Now it's 85 for women and 81 for men. When guys were living until 72 it made sense to get a job and stay with it through retirement. Now that they are living almost a decade longer the "post-work" life isn't necessarily about relaxing and playing golf: it is about continuing your legacy in different ways.

Technology's Dark Side That Needs To Be Addressed

As Spiderman says "with great power comes great responsibility"... at least he knew it. The excitement of being able to do great work in the world comes with the burden of doing it well. Having said that, it's a lot easier to live with the belief that "life happens to us" as opposed to "life happens for us" merely because the latter demands that we take responsibility for our choices and actions and trust that in all situations there is an opportunity for growth or gratitude. We live in a world in which people are constantly switched on, allowing life to happen to them. They don't even know where to start to reflect, process and integrate into their lives what can truly serve them.

All along we have been carrying immense power in our connected portable devices: power to access information at any time, launch and build brands, share content almost as quickly as you can think it into existence and reach mass audiences at any time. We've also been growing a mass epidemic of what we can call narcissistic personality trait disorder (NPTD) by giving people the ability to gain questionable validation and a sense of false belonging through likes and comments on social media posts. Whether a person is being truthful or not is irrelevant.

The growing trend for validation outside the self is leading to a false sense of what really matters if you want to lead a life that's worthwhile and aligned to your purpose. In a recent study of mental health around the world, Sapien Labs found that 44% of 18-24 year-olds in internet-enabled countries were distressed or very stressed about their "social self" and had obsessive thoughts about their status, comparison anxiety, self-blame and guilt. With our technology metaphorically (for now) "attached" to our bodies through habituated behaviors, we as a society by and large have been forming the "always on" culture whether we wanted to or not. This awareness requires us to take a step back and reclaim a deeper sense of meaning in our lives while using technology to serve the evolution of humanity and our planet for the greater good.

These current macro views of the state of the world suggest why we need to exercise agency to create things that matter in our lives and why we need to question everything to gain a deeper sense of awareness of the self and those around us. Related issues include:

- Polarity Amplified

  The overworked brain is always looking to save energy and one of the key ways of doing this is through binary thinking: it's either A or B. Combine that with social media encouraging cognitive bias through it's algorithms, facilitating highly stimulated opposing "tribes" and we have polarity: right or left, black or white, cryptocurrency or fiat and the list goes on. A solution mindset frames the conversation which is then deferred until the right solution apparently comes along. Might we be open to both sides having viable arguments, neither being viable, taking the middle ground or staying open to a novel possibility on the way we perceive something?

- Positive Intelligence Economy

The "be positive" movement has counter-produced generations that overlooked emotions of discomfort. They lacked tools to face these less pleasurable emotions head on, dismissing the notion that processing heavier feelings and practicing consistent healing are vital paths to cultivating sustained inner peace, gratitude, joy and a sense of anti-fragility. Positive psychology, mainly introduced by Martin Seligman as President of the American Psychological Association to use psychological resources to look at good outcomes and not just mental illness, has been misinterpreted. Life's not about being positive it's about being adaptive. There's a big difference in the connotations of those words.

Healthy adaptation represents meaningful resilience that goes beyond the "I". However, the default position of many people is to deny responsibility and justify anything that works for them. Examples include:

- Planetary Negligence

    "It's not that important if it doesn't affect me directly." Now it is affecting more of us directly, from the fires in Colorado, USA and in the Amazon rainforest, flash floods in Bangladesh and heat waves across Europe.

- The Great Search for Purpose

Caused by economic volatility fueled by COVID, non-conformist uprisings due to increased state-enforced regulations on employees, the "be my own boss" movement, the precariousness of work and the exploitation of workers who in many countries don't have any social benefits like health care and rise of the entrepreneurial spirit.

- Rampant Burnout

    Blended work and personal lifestyles are creating blurred boundaries and requiring self-monitoring to avoid burnout due to too much work, family or on the flipside being so overwhelmed, using "self-love" as an escape instead of addressing the root cause of burnout in the first place. In addition, the tendency of us being excessive has increased and calling oneself out is becoming more crucial than ever before.

- Exponential Technologies

    Cryptocurrency is challenging traditional financial systems. AI is challenging the way we work, our educational systems and more. Blockchain is challenging the concept of authority and governance. And many others, each of which follows the exponential growth curve.

The 6Ds of Exponential Growth is a framework developed by Peter Diamandis that describes a chain reaction of technological progress that leads to upheaval and opportunity. The model consists of six stages: Digitization, Deception, Disruption, Demonetization, Dematerialization, and Democratization.

The first stage, Digitization, involves taking a product or service and turning it into digital data. The second stage, Deception, is about exploring the potential for disruption and identifying any limitations or obstacles that may arise. The third stage, Disruption, involves introducing the product or service to the market and causing significant changes to the industry. The fourth stage, Demonetization, is about making the product or service more affordable and accessible to the masses. The fifth stage, Dematerialization, involves reducing the amount of physical resources needed to produce the product or service. The final stage, Democratization, is about making the product or service available to everyone, regardless of their background or location.

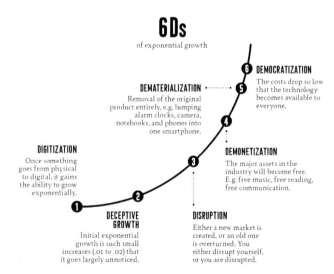

(Source: Abundance by Peter Diamandis & Steven Kotler)

- Mental Health Crisis

  A sense of isolation in a world of hyper-connectedness is a bizarre situation we find ourselves in, with several factors at play. This can stem from one's digital identity being far different to their reality, leading to a shunning away real life situations to hide behind a screen. It may also have to do with the automation of our world that requires less human interaction and calls for more screen time through gamified apps that feed our dopamine desires. According to the National Institute of Mental Health Disorders, depression is one of the leading causes of disability. Suicide is the fourth leading cause of death among 15-29 year-olds. People with severe mental health conditions die prematurely – as much as two decades early – due to preventable physical conditions.

- The Escape Culture

  A $3 trillion industry globally shows that people are seeking ways to cope or put a pause on their productivity to revitalize their creativity as highlighted in the book Stealing Fire by Steven Kolter & Jamie Wheal.

- The Repackaging of Ancient Wisdom

  With the increased popularity of better self-regulation with biofeedback devices, mindful movement gaining popularity with the reemergence of communities who practice yoga, transcendental meditation, plant medicine and the likes springing up across the globe. Mind, body and soul retreats and online courses on how to live better, tribal music festivals and regenerative agriculture movements; we can see many ways in which the perspectives of our ancestors are regaining importance in our busy lives if we are to manage these global shifts with strength, antifragility and grace.

- Awakening Into Purpose and Intentional Living

   To truly find out who we are and how we want to develop a legacy that is beneficial for all we must stop and breathe: stop to recognize the automatic perceptions and behaviors that have become ingrained into our identity while we weren't looking and then breathe to look inside and find out who we really are, what we really want and what we can give back.

If you think of your life from a higher perspective, the last moment in life might never come. This life on this planet as we know it might be a tiny snapshot of a higher, greater, bigger journey of your human existence regardless of which belief system you hold on the meaning of life, whether you consider yourself spiritual, atheist, religious or not; acknowledging this possibility means the journey never ends, or as Simon Sinek puts it, we're here to play the infinite game. If that's the case, the remaining time you have should be used to honor the greatness of the creation that you represent, just for being here, now. Honoring each minute, every breath and every heartbeat will give you a sense of self-ownership and accountability with The Creator; or if that's too much for you to swallow, imagine you're playing the infinite game towards your ultimate self-expression and the body-suit you're in will only last so long. So love this life, live loving and just be there for yourself in all moments in life.

The remainder of this playbook explores these concepts and how we can awaken to a new reality which will give you more power and purpose than you might have ever imagined.

References

Jamie Wheal (2021) Recapture the Rapture: Rethinking God, Sex, and Death in a World That's Lost Its Mind. Harper Wave.

Peter H. Diamandis and Steven Kotler (2012) Abundance: The Future Is Better Than You Think

Simon Sinek (2019) The Infinite Game

Steven Kolter & Jamie Wheal (2017) Stealing Fire

Jennifer Moss. (2021) Beyond Burned Out. Harvard Business Review. https://hbr.org/2021/02/beyond-burned-out

Jennifer Newson, Oleksii Sukhoi, Joseph Taylor, Olesia Topalo & Tara Thiagarajan. (2022) The Mental State of the World Report 2021. https://sapienlabs.org/all-publications-results/?topic=mentalstateoftheworld

Francisco Palao, Michelle Lapierre & Salim Ismail. (2019). Exponential Transformation: Evolve Your Organization (and Change the World) with a 10-Week ExO Sprint. John Wiley & Sons.

Links

Peter Diamandis. *The 6Ds of Exponential Growth.*
https://www.diamandis.com/blog/the-6ds#:~:text=This%20growth%20cycle%20takes%20place,demonetization%2C%20dematerialization%2C%20and%20democratization.&text=This%20opens%20in%20a%20new,an%20exponential%20technology%20is%20born.

Chapter 2

Who is an Exponential Individual?

"Give out everything you came with. Don't remain in your comfort zone full of potential only to die with them unused."
— *Clement Ogedegbe*

Contributors: Ann Boothello, Eric Patel, Howard Rankin

Here are some ways to describe An Exponential Individual.

An Exponential Individual is someone whose impact for good and level of fulfillment is disproportionately large compared to her/his peers because of evolved thoughts, behaviors and actions that leverage everything within and around her/him.

An Exponential Individual is someone whose impact and level of achievement are disproportionately large compared to the effort, and resources put into their actions and projects due to alignment to their purpose.

They are people who show up in a new way of being.

An Exponential Individual is someone who has habituated accessing and managing their human potential to be their best, moment by moment. She/he is someone who harnesses her innate human potential and makes a massive impact on others and the world while living a fulfilling life. She/he uses her/his virtues and purpose(s) to help guide her/his life.

Exponential Individuals are people who go beyond the "I," they are passionate about seeing their loved ones and society live more fulfilling lives and experience the best version of themselves in their lifetime.

Common characteristics of exponential individuals include:

- Mindset
    - Exercising mental fitness
    - Can-do attitude
    - Growth mindset
    - Abundance
    - Mental wellbeing
    - State management
    - Self-regulation
    - Active listening

- Heart-set
    - Authenticity
    - Emotional intelligence
    - Love-based decision-making
    - Vulnerability
    - Honesty
    - Empathy
    - Compassion
    - Collaboration
    - Gratitude

- Self-awareness
    - Living by their values
    - Being courageous
    - Trusting intuition

- Becoming the best version of yourself
- Being in the present
- Self-love ie. "oxygen mask on first"

- Purpose-driven: Their actions are driven by their inner purpose(s) to create a meaningful life.

- Personal values: They constantly build their character and live by their values based on what resonates with them such as curiosity/wonder, love, leadership, honesty, humility, courage; they provide value in the world by living true to their values.

- Universal values: They contribute to something bigger than themselves such as the possibility of abundance for all, positive evolution of our collective, leaving a legacy to benefit future generations, and/or belief in a higher power/spirituality/energy as a guiding force.

- Personal development/self-improvement/personal success: They are committed to continuous improvement and lifelong learning; perfection is never the goal, however betterment is.

- Flow: They experience flow states where action can take place without conscious effort.

- Community-minded: They are actively involved with participating in and contributing to communities; power of the collective; co-creating shared value in a collective; they encourage multiple voices/input to add value/solve problems, freely share knowledge and insights.

- Doer, action-taker: They serve with an entrepreneurial spirit being problem-solvers, risk-takers, creative thinkers, blending pragmatic thinking with intuitive action; they make ongoing contributions, are not afraid to speak up and make a difference.

Key ExI Attributes

- Awareness: of the self, those around them and the universe
- Presence: know that their power lies in the present moment
- Compassion: concern for another's suffering
- Inner Purpose: a sense of "why" one does what they do
- Fulfillment: attaining self-actualization
- Self-determination: strong will to do what one needs to do
- Sense of Agency: Acting purposefully without delay
- Upskilling for better leadership of one's life: evolving for the better
- Upskilling for a transformational technological era: embracing the power of technology for good
- Personal effectiveness: working smarter, not harder
- Contribution to community: giving back in service of others
- Desire to create a masterpiece of one's work: belief in oneself to produce great work
- Likely to participate in solving one or more of our world's grand challenges: a sense of responsibility for collective & planetary betterment
- Positively impacting the world through their way of being: embodying the ExI attributes so as to lead by example
- Explore their ability to be limitless: curious about their ability to be and serve more

- Flow between surrender and control: grounded enough to gracefully take life's situations as teachers for growth and/or gratitude and disciplined enough to know what's needed to be done in the moment
- Deeply believing they can achieve anything and do so, despite the odds, more times than not: often challenge the status quo
- Quick to pivot when faced with a setback: they know failure is needed for their evolution, not attached to the outcome
- Harnessing her/his abundant human potential: has enough self-awareness to know how to leverage their natural abilities and inner power
- Learning the art of optimizing their way of being to create desired life experiences: master manifestors
- Expressing the greatest version of oneself: authentically show up through the process of becoming

How does one become an Exponential Individual? This lifelong journey, while fraught with challenges, temptations and excuses, is ultimately possible. Here's one possible pathway to becoming an ExI:

1. Visualize and describe the person you want to become
2. Discover your reason(s) for being: your inner purpose(s)
3. Actively engage with relevant communities organized around human transformation
4. Find an accountability buddy and/or advisory team
5. Achieve self-improvement by setting objectives and tracking your key results (OKRs) or identifying your key performance indicators (KPIs)

6. Define your range: minimum viable standard (MVS) vs. the optimal version of you
7. Validate what works for you through deliberate practice
8. Tap into and manage your human potential, moment by moment
9. Consistently self-reflect to become self-aware
10. Evolve in a manner that sustains the gains for the long term
11. Start the process of collective engagement and encourage feedback loops

Connecting With Your Entire Self: The Power Of Play

Remember when you were a child and you played alone or with friends? Your curiosity as yet unconstrained by cultural perceptions and limited stereotypes helped you learn how to do things better, to create, to relate to others and your environment. You were fascinated by and played with little things: frost on a window, butterflies and grasshoppers, rocks and shells. You were full of excitement when a friend came over to play because you could both escape to an imagined global adventure or a simple hide-and-seek game. Pets were like people. Toys had personalities. Your imagination was almost as exciting as real events.

Unfortunately, as we grew into adults, responsibilities, socially-constructed roles, problems, difficulties and the need to 'make money' all took over - and their toll on us. We lost connection with our inner child and the ability to see the world as it could or should be.

We are here to remind you that the "power of play" is real and still within you even if dormant. The adult-disillusioned perspective of life is misleading. It's a mask covering your true nature to play. By reconnecting with the power of play you can transform your world into a better future. When you know what to do to bring forward the power of play you will start to live the life of your dreams and wonder how you ever gave up believing in the power of play. Are you ready to experience play again? Are you ready to be fulfilled every day like when you were a child?

This may be very hard to discern for yourself. The answer lies in peeling back layers of adult social constructs of what is real while being careful not to dispel them completely as they help you function in your world right now but to recognize them for what they are: beliefs that can be shaped to better serve you, your family, your community and your world.

If you do the work and discover your inner play you may discover that your current roles, relationships, circumstances are not in alignment with your ability to "play at your best". The hardest part is facing and dealing with the consequences of your awareness. So, this is not a journey for the faint of heart: it's a journey for the brave, the courageous and the adventurous to re-discover their inner child.

What is the ExI Playbook?

The playbook recognizes common problems faced by humanity such as:

- Lack of wellness and well-being.
- Burnout, anxiety, depression and other threats to personal wellness.

- Instant gratification and escapism.
- Lack of emotional intelligence for oneself and others.
- Fear/scarcity mentality.
- Unhealthy relationships.
- Lack of desire, interest or willpower to become your best, leading to unfulfilled lives.
- Social hypnosis.
- Simply going through the motions, living in autopilot / cruise control / "zombie mode".
- Diminished human potential (effectiveness, efficiency, productivity and/or performance).
- Not exploring how thinking, consciousness and the subconscious really work.
- Rampant time-wasting and misprioritization on what's really important.
- Lack of concern and action on what really matters to evolve as a human species into a fairer, freer and harmonized society.
- Lack of a unified sense of agency towards fulfilling purpose and extending care.

Do you know what your limits really are? In his book *The Way of the Seal*, Ret. U.S. Navy Seal Commander Mark Divine has a chapter titled "Find Your 20x Factor" which is all about embracing a personal culture of mighty effort. You may be surprised to find out that you have more in you than you think you do and that you have what it takes to overcome any challenge.

The ExI Playbook contains several pathways for you to exceed even your own wildest expectations, optimize your human potential and show you possible pathways for you to be at your best, moment by moment. It is not an instruction manual: it's a cookbook of sorts with different recipes because one size does not fit all. It's less prescriptive and more free-flowing to allow anyone to pick-and-choose a path to pursue.

The ExI Playbook gives tribute to ancient wisdom along with modern science and the freedom of choice to achieve one's full self-expression. The playbook gives any reader the space to explore the infinite possibilities that lie within them as they remember that their mind, body, heart and soul are their greatest gifts. It is structured starting with big-picture, strategic views and becomes more tactical and practical in subsequent chapters. Each chapter builds upon previous ones.

We encourage you to have a notebook at your side to journal and answer the guided questions in the chapter.

Each chapter exercises and resources for you to continue along your journey. The playbook is not meant to be something that you simply read cover-to-cover and put back on the shelf. In order to fully embrace becoming an Exponential Individual there is much work to do; we say this with caution, because we do believe when you are in alignment work even though extremely challenging at times can more times that not, feel like play! Change and investments of time and effort, perhaps even money, are required. In the end, not only will you benefit but the people in your life, your community and the world will also be positively influenced by your way of being. The world, as you know it, will ultimately be a better place.

Case Study

Onyema was a young girl living in a poor village in Nigeria. Her grandmother was her primary caregiver as her mother was often in a neighboring village selling her goods while her father was no longer around. When she was a young girl, Onyema saw a plane fly overhead for the first time. The sight inspired her. She decided that one day she would fly a plane.

Her chances to realize her dream were not good: she lived in a poor area with minimal education and there was no money in the family that could fund her travel and years of education and training. Luckily children don't preoccupy themselves with such concerns.

She excelled at school especially in science which was typically restricted to boys, and one day as she neared graduation she took a ten-hour bus ride to a town that had internet. She researched different schools that offered aeronautical programs. She applied to take the Scholastic Aptitude Test (SAT) and when she scored well, she applied to the University of Alabama. She didn't even realize she would need money to submit her SAT application but two guys at the internet café who were also investigating the SAT gave her what she needed.

She was accepted at the Alabama school at Tuscaloosa. When she flew to the USA she landed in Atlanta without realizing she needed another flight to Tuscaloosa. Again, she found herself short on funds but a Nigerian couple on the flight with her lent her the money so she could continue on to her final destination.

She completed her education semester by semester since she needed time to earn money to pay for each semester. She ended up studying at six different schools including Harvard University.

She eventually graduated and became an aeronautical engineer. Today she is a major advocate for girls who wish to study Science, Technology, Engineering, Mathematics (STEM) subjects around the world including her home country.

Who is the ExI Playbook's intended audience?

While anyone is capable of becoming an Exponential Individual, not everyone will. Why not? Like forming any habit, one initially needs an extended period of time dedicated to overcoming one's "old" self. This requires a level of compassion and understanding for one's own unique growth process and the ability to celebrate wins along the way even if the only person at the party is you. It requires discipline in following through to becoming the best version of yourself regardless of challenges and setbacks.

The ExI Playbook is for anyone who feels stuck in her/his current stage of life where she needs inspiration on how to move ahead with confidence and excitement. Whether you know what your north star/inner purpose is or not, committing to the journey often needs to be done several times throughout the process of self-actualization. It's normal for us to give up when things seem too tough to handle. Yet, with repetitive commitment to personal mastery that too can become something you can overcome.

Recent research has divided the workforce into those who believe in the "fit" theory and those who believe in the "develop" theory.

The "fit" theorists would endorse the following statement:

- I believe that there is a perfect job fit for every individual and finding the right line of work will determine one's happiness and success at work.

The "develop" theorists, in contrast, are more likely to agree with statements such as:

- I believe that passion is developed through a learning process within any chosen line of work. The better one gets at one's type of work, the more one will start to love the profession.

In the words of BBC work/life journalist David Robson:

"The fit theorists will struggle to find happiness in a job that doesn't meet their specific criteria. The develop theorists, in contrast, can learn to find enjoyment and interest in the different tasks, so that their satisfaction grows over time, even if the job didn't initially tick all the desired boxes."

In a research paper by Chen et al., (2021) they compare how these different mindsets affect the search for meaning.

"A "develop" mindset about passion is the belief that passion is developed over time toward a career or subject major. This is contrasted with a "fit" mindset about passion, which is the belief that passion is found through the fit with the "right" career or subject major. These mindsets about passion have important implications for people's expectations, choices, and well-being (Chen et al., 2015). Prior studies on mindsets of passion, which primarily studied working adults, found that working adults who endorsed a "develop" mindset (more so than a "fit" mindset) forecasted that their passion toward an unenjoyable line of work would grow over time. Hence, these adults were less inclined to prioritize immediate enjoyment in a line of work and preferred other important vocational characteristics such as pay. In contrast, working adults who endorsed the "fit" mindset (over the develop mindset) expected their passion toward a job to remain high over time, hence they tended to prioritize immediate enjoyment over other vocational characteristics when choosing a job. Both the "develop" and "fit" mindsets significantly predicted people's self-reported vocational passion, satisfaction, and commitment toward their vocations – indicating that people with either dominant mindset are able to achieve passion toward their work, just through different means (Chen and Ellaworth, 2019)."

In one study these researchers found that students who increased their passion did so through several means:

"(a) recognizing personal relevance in learning the subject, (b) recognizing the societal relevance of the subject, (c) building familiarity with the subject, (d) gaining practical experience in applying the subject, (e) seeking or recognizing the influence of teachers or environments, (f) focusing on parts of the subject that they naturally like, and (g) performing well in the subject."

Whether you have a "develop" or "fit" mindset, this book will give you tools to discover your purpose.

The playbook is intended to help people coach themselves into living an optimal life. It is intended to guide anyone who is deeply curious on how to consistently improve their lives authentically and aligned with their highest purpose.

Exercises

1. Reflect in your journal your personal takeaways from this chapter.
2. How do you define an Exponential Individual?
3. Do you know anyone who is living an exponential life?
4. Describe a time when you have exceeded your expectations in some way.
   a. If so, why did that happen?
   b. If so, how did that happen?
5. Do you consider yourself to be exponential? Why or why not?
6. What would you have to know, be or do for you to consider yourself to be exponential?

References

Chen P, Lin Y, Pereira DJH, O'Keefe PA and Yates JF (2021) Fanning the Flames of Passion: A Develop Mindset Predicts Strategy-Use Intentions to Cultivate Passion. Front. Psychol. 12:634903. doi: 10.3389/fpsyg.2021.634903

Mark Devine. (2018) *The Way of the Seal: Think Like an Elite Warrior to Lead and Succeed.* Trusted Media. Expanded edition.

Bill Burnett and Dave Evans (2016) *Designing Your Life. How to Build a Well-Lived, Joyful Life.* Knopf

Lynda Gratton and Andrew Scott. (2018) *The 100 year life. Living and Working in the Age of Longevity.* Bloomsbury Press.

Jon Simpson. (2017) Finding Brand Success in the Digital World. Forbes. August 25, 2017.

Links

David Robson. BBC Worklife.
https://www.bbc.com/worklife/article/20230113-the-mindset-to-re-kindle-lost-passion

Lynda Gratton The Shift (the future of work)
https://youtu.be/6Z6L7iZlC9o   ;
https://lyndagratton.com/thinking/the-future-of-work

https://www.forbes.com/sites/forbesagencycouncil/2017/08/25/finding-brand-success-in-the-digital-world/?sh=5e9162e2626e

https://www.youtube.com/watch?v=tgyXue8-jXw&t=442s

Yuval Noah Harari, 60 Minutes interview,
https://www.youtube.com/watch?v=EIVTf-C6oQo

Chapter 3

Life, Death and Consciousness

"If you live without awareness, it is the same as being dead. You cannot call that kind of existence being alive. Many of us live like dead people because we live without awareness. We carry our dead bodies with us and circulate throughout the world. We are pulled into the past or we are pulled forward into the future or we are caught by our projects or our despair and anger. We are not truly alive; we are not inhabited by awareness of the miracle of being alive."
— *Thich Nhất Hạnh*

Contributors: Ann Boothello, Eric Patel, Howard Rankin

Thich Nhat Hanh was a Vietnamese Buddhist monk who passed away on the 22nd of January 2022. He was one of the world's most influential Zen masters spreading messages of mindfulness, compassion and nonviolence while promoting the ability, necessity and importance of recognizing and moving beyond our habitual perceptions. This message introduces this section of the playbook and lays the foundation for the rest of the guidance contained within.

The depth to which an individual goes to find the meaning of life, death and consciousness depends on several factors.

One outlook often shared by life coach, author, entrepreneur and philanthropist Tony Robbins' is that "life happens for us, not to us." This is easier to believe when things are going well rather than when things aren't going well. Nevertheless, if you believe that the universe, God, divine, higher intelligence, the creators of the infinite game or whatever you believe in has our best interests at heart and that what you experience in life is a series of events which you may not understand nor agree with but ultimately will serve you, then your whole perspective and outlook change for the better.

Similarly, Michael Singer in his book *The Surrender Experiment* talks about what happens when you let the flow of life be in charge of your existence, when you disregard your own personal preferences, likes and dislikes and instead look to see what is being asked of you as each situation unfolds. Singer found that the constant act of letting go of one's self-centered thoughts and emotions was all that was needed for profound personal, professional and spiritual growth.

Earl Nightingale in his 1956 audio recording called *The Strangest Secret* discovered something so simple yet so ignored: we become what we think about most of the time. Thoughts, in fact, are things which can be manifested in your life.

We should be open to accepting alternative views on the meaning of life.

Why are we here? Good question. Let's consider various viewpoints from people from all walks of life and times:

- Experience life fully
- Self-mastery
- Love one another.
- Help others.
- Learn lesson(s).
- Serve others.
- "Get it right" or you'll keep coming back until you do.
- Karma
- Contribute to collective betterment

These notions aren't mutually exclusive. Brian Johnson in his Optimize Coach program has stated his belief of what we should be doing: "master ourselves, serve heroically, empower others to do the same;" so we can change the world, one person at a time, together, starting with you and me, today. Simply put: to live expressing the best version of yourself moment by moment, to flourish, to live with values/virtues and serve the world, living heroically.

Who We Really Are

We are a meaning-making species whether we are aware of it or not. Every situation in our life either creates new patterns of thought, emotion and behavior or reinforces old ones. Some of these patterns serve our evolution for the better while others hinder our way of experiencing present moments and as a result, obstruct our journey to authentic fulfillment.

As a meaning-making species we create stories to help us navigate the world we live in: stories of our childhood, our past relationships, jobs, trauma and triumphs. We've got a hero and villain in them all and we choose which role we play whether we play the victim, villain or hero. Depending on whether we believe we have the power to change the character roles we once played, we either move forward with confidence that we can play the game differently next time with the will to do better or we use the jadedness of a disturbing outcome to stay in a self-sabotaging loop: that if it happened once it will happen again so why bother doing better? The more we hold attachment to stories we create, good or bad, the less breathing room we leave for the evolution of the self into its truest, greatest expression. This evolution is not just about removing negative beliefs; it's also about improving our positive self-beliefs. It's important though that when we shift out of stories that don't serve us, that we learn how to digest the grief or anger that may be associated with it. How? Look up ways to process anger & grief and try what feels right for you; there are multiple pathways to re-writing a better story. Some include: "rage on a page" where you journal out your anger fully, yes fully, no holding back. Another may be releasing the pain from your body - crying, often seen as weak, is a great release and shows one's strength in exercising vulnerability instead of holding back the tears as many of us were once thought to do. Similarly screaming into a pillow, or doing a high-intensity workout can help "blow some steam," dropping our cortisol levels (stress hormones) and encouraging our nervous system to get back into equilibrium.

Findings in neuroscience shows us that 95% of who we are by the age of 35 is a memorized set of behaviors, emotional reactions and hardwired attitudes. Memories create neural pathways in the brain. The more impactful the memory (the greater the emotion) or the more times it was repeated, the more likely you are to remember it because the circuits, or neural pathways created, are reinforced as a prominent memory of your past. The end product of each memory of your past is an emotion and it is through that emotion that you give meaning to the experience and craft a story to help you either cope, protect yourself from or recreate something similar in the future.

How can we create a future we want for ourselves if we're making decisions in the present with reference to our past? If how we think and how we feel reflect our current way of being and if we are constantly using our "predictable past" as Dr. Joe Dispenza states, to create our future, how can we create a new model of living that allows for a more promising future for ourselves, our loved ones and the collective? The questions are: Are these stories empowering or stifling? Why do we hold on to old stories to guide us on how to act now?

Maybe detachment from our past to create anew, as practiced in Buddhism, is the way for some. Maybe crafting beautiful stories from a troubling past is the way for others. Ultimately, those who use their past stories to make better choices or those who detach from stories altogether have one thing in common: they embody the practice of thinking greater than the emotions of their past, in the now, without discrediting the way they feel in the moment. Rather, they observe it and choose to think differently. They learn the art of generating new empowering thoughts that create a better feeling emotion that leads to acting in accordance with the part of the self that wants better, moment by moment.

We are intrigued by the notion of being the architect of our emotions. Scientist and author Lisa Fieldman Barrett has dedicated her life's work to the scientific study of emotions. She states that we can use them as a tool that serves us and that even in extreme emotional states, one should question oneself on the root cause. Could I turn down the dial of this emotional state? Could this be because of a purely physical habit, lack of sleep or a nutrition deficiency? Or is it because of the meaning I'm making or the story I'm creating? What can I do about it?

Let's start with one of the simple tools available to all of us: the ability to practice gratitude in the now. Gratitude is one of the quickest ways to shift uncomfortable emotions. Gratitude for what you may ask, when you may not be feeling your best? Gratitude, that you are *allowing* yourself the space to feel the difficult emotions. From one industrial revolution to the next, we've applauded those who make their way through life "efficiently" like "machines" getting things done, and shunned those who stopped to honor the needs of their emotional body, intuitive mind and free spirit. By allowing yourself the right of passage to feel uncomfortable emotions, we can build our antifragile mental muscle and a heart-set that's un-jaded that allows us to look at adversity as a path to greater wisdom.

Nasseb Taleb defines being antifragile as "representing things that benefit from disorder." Notice that we did not say dismiss uncomfortable emotions; we said acknowledge them. In other words, move through them and use them as fuel for your fire. And yes, maybe even be grateful for them since every emotion can guide us into taking an intelligent or intuitive next step, whether good or bad. In fact, emotions themselves are not good or bad; they are indications that something important is happening. They are better described not in a moral way (good or bad) but in an experiential way: comfortable or uncomfortable.

With the awareness and knowledge that we are not victims of our emotions but instead can use them to self-author our lives. This brings us to a core revelation that we believe may be a key reason for humanity and our planet's current state of unhealed brokenness: the association of burden placed on the act of taking responsibility. This applies to ourselves, the collective and our planet.

If I'm responsible for my own emotions, who or what else can I blame? No one and nothing. This does not disregard that there aren't people doing "bad" things to other people and we should excuse them for it. But rather, this proposes that, regardless of what is going on in our surroundings, we have the ability to make meaning out of it to serve us or embrace the emotion, change the thought in the moment and allow for a new emotion to emerge. What if we rethought responsibility for our thoughts, emotions, behaviors and attitudes as an act of service to ourselves? What if this self-responsibility could be viewed as self-love, giving us a reason for being and the ability to take back our power to shape our lives for the better?

"You are not required to finish your work, yet neither are you permitted to desist from it." This is from Pirke Aboth, which translates as "The Ethics of the Fathers" consisting of ethical teachings of the Rabbinic Jewish tradition.

Or as Viktor Frankl wrote:

"Everything can be taken from a man but one thing: the last of the human freedoms—to choose one's attitude in any given set of circumstances, to choose one's own way."

Between making the thought of self-responsibility an act of self-love through empowering meaning-making of our lives or hand-picking thoughts to shift our state and becoming masters of our emotions, we've got our work cut out to set the foundations. However, this is what is needed for us to confront the bigger question: what can be done to create the future we want not just for ourselves but for those we love and the greater good?

Author Rhonda Byrne of the *The Secret* book series wrote in her book *The Greatest Secret* that we are nothing more than eternal/infinite awareness/consciousness. Feeling good is our true nature. All that really exists is this present moment.

Truths, Beliefs, Virtues and Values

What we come to believe is usually a function of our social identities, context and influences. We are each taught from the time we are born and throughout our lives the "norms" of making sense of and reacting to our own perceptions and emotions. We each construct our own version of reality mostly unconsciously based on these learned behaviors and what is repeatedly modeled for us.

Our capacity to consciously observe and reconsider these mental models for ourselves is called individuation in which we, to varying degrees, develop a more intentional self-identity and modes of self-expression. However, this is the work that we each would do well if we hope to shine a light of awareness on our habits of mind. That is how we habitually make sense of our own perceptions and emotions, circumstances and events. So irrespective of one's apparent personal truth and beliefs, we each have them usually unconsciously and by default. The invitation is to do the work to uncover what's present by way of our mental habits and their impact and then engage in conscious sensemaking in which we literally rewire how we parse the meaning of our moment to moment realities.

We have to recognize the social influence on our constructs. We know they are constructs because they have changed over time. In addition, what is socially acceptable varies by culture. Think about how different cultures have views/laws on childbirth, marriage, voting, work hours and education, to name a few.

Fear-based vs. love-inspired decision-making

There is a depth and complexity to life that we cannot dismiss, yet to live well in the present moment requires us to strip away unnecessary complexity that can impede our progress and arrive at simple-enough solutions on what the next best step to take is. We are problem-solving and adaptive beings. The question is whether we are arriving at solutions based on fear of breaking away from the comfort of past experiences and/or a sense of wonder for the possibilities that lie ahead.

Being aware or conscious of whether a decision or solution you have arrived at is fear-based or love-inspired is the litmus test we can use to help us catalyze our ongoing progress in a direction that is positive to our growth and aligned to our purpose(s.) Instead of repeating a pattern that keeps you stuck perhaps you can see and execute an alternative path free from habitual thinking and social influences.

This goes for basic, everyday decisions such as how many cups of coffee you consume daily or whom you choose to partner with for your next entrepreneurial venture. Of course, some decisions weigh heavier than others and need more consideration, but the process you follow is the same. Characteristics of fear-based vs. love-inspired decision-making include:

Fear-Based	Love-Inspired
Constricted feeling	Expansive feeling
Habits that don't serve us	Habits that serve us
Negative self-talk	Empowering self-talk
Isolation	Connection & community
Ego ("Me") - Self-orientation	We-Go ("Us") - Collective-orientation

There are decision-making tools one can use:

- Weight of the question, problem or situation at hand: Tim Ferris had a good suggestion on how to think about this. He suggested we ask ourselves the question: "What are the stakes?" In other words, what are the possible consequences with regard to impact on my life? Choosing which brand of clothing to buy vs. the person you want to spend the rest of your life with should be approached with the appropriate level of attention.

- Worst-case scenario thinking: Tim Ferris also has another tool called the Fear-Setting Exercise to put your fears under the microscope and gain clarity on their perceived impact. The greater the emotional reaction, the more energy needs to be spent on reaching the right path forward.

- Intuition: Tapping into intuition stems from a person's understanding of what their heart feels about a situation. Often, when one talks about living optimally, the mindset is the first matter at hand. However, if one does not know the direction they wish to go in, what use is the mind in optimally actioning progress? The analogy of "barking up the wrong tree" is the outcome of a person who has lost a deeper connection with their heart, their sense of knowing, their inner guidance on where to go and what to do. This can also translate to people who do not act on their intuitive nudges because they feel it may not be rational enough. Often this is seen as heart versus mind when instead it should be heart and mind. Indeed, in their recent book *Intuitive Rationality* Grant Renier and Howard Rankin point out that data and logic are important but are often devoid of context and that the combination of intuition and data is needed to make successful predictions and decisions. For example, if the chance of you being involved in a car accident on a Tuesday is about 10,000 to 1, you still need to swerve to avoid that oncoming car that ran the red light every Tuesday and every other day.

Practicing Presence or Finding Stillness Within

A core skill to cultivate for anyone who wants to tap into their infinite potential is the ability to find stillness in our days. Some call this the practice of mindfulness or meditation, breathwork or quiet observation. Although there are numerous ways of developing this skill, the essential learning is the ability to suspend one's analytical mind and experience the moment at hand, without preconceptions, for what it is. The art of being present to *observe* a moment as it unfolds is where we can experience life more fully.

As Vago and Silberswieg write in their 2012 article on the neurobiological basis of mindfulness:

"Although the contemporary view of the concept, "mindfulness" is increasingly becoming part of popular culture, there remains no single "correct" or "authoritative version" of mindfulness and the concept is often trivialized and conflated with many common interpretations. Mindfulness is described as (1) A temporary state of non-judgmental, non-reactive, present-centered attention and awareness that is cultivated during meditation practice; (2) An enduring trait that can be described as a dispositional pattern of cognition, emotion, or behavioral tendency; (3) A meditation practice; (4) An intervention."

Looking at the world through filters we've developed from our past experiences is called "top-down" processing: when we do so, we already have an idea of what we are seeing, because we use our preconceived ideas to make sense of the moment.

Bottom-up processing involves focusing on your experience of what is in front of you, not what you expect to be in front of you. This takes a lot of practice but is essential. It is the way to minimize the cultural, habitual processes that may not serve in your positive evolution. Your view of the world and of yourself is bound to feel more expansive and moldable as you practice this.

The continued practice of being fully present in each moment through habituating mindfulness practices and mindfulness/meditation has shown to have several major effects: improved attention, emotional regulation, extinction and reconsolidation of negative narratives, prosocial cognition and non-attachment to the concept of self.

Research done by Johns Hopkins University has shown that there is a direct correlation with the ability to be still through meditation specifically causing our immunoglobulin count to increase and our cortisol levels to drop: thus one improves immunity and reduces stress. These psychological (mind) and physiological (body) benefits are just some of what developing a habit that invokes more presence, stillness or mindfulness can do.

"Mindfulness meditation is a form of present moment awareness," explains Neda Gould, Ph.D., associate director of the Johns Hopkins Bayview Medical Center Anxiety Disorders Clinic and head of a mindfulness program at the Johns Hopkins University School of Medicine. "It's about paying attention in the present moment — to what is here — in a nonjudgmental way without fixating on the past or dwelling on the future."

"This form of insight demonstrates that there is no truly existing self (i.e., subject) that continues through life without change and provides the practitioner with the critical distinction between the phenomenological experience of oneself and one's thoughts, emotions, and feelings that appear "thing-like" (Varela et al., 1991). This realization of impermanence of all "thing-like" objects including the self is also described as a "release from mental fixations," or" non-attachment."

Exercises

1.   Focused Attention

There are many different ways of practicing presence and developing a sense of mindfulness exercises. But the key skill is switching off the habitual editors or filters in your head and moving from top-down to bottom-up processing. This is a change in your brain activity.

When you are in processing mode you have a lot of beta wave activity in your brain. Beta waves range from 12-30 Hz. As beta activity increases within this range, your mental state goes from healthy levels of stress to anxiety to chronic stress to obsessive disorders to becoming delusional.

Theta waves of 4-8 Hz reflect very relaxed wakefulness when the brain "slows down" and you are able to experience rather than think.

Let's start with the simple and largely unacknowledged importance of the act of breathing. Conscious breathing is where you can start on the mindfulness and higher consciousness journey. Benefits include:

Self-regulation: Lowering of heart rate, over time lowering of cortisol (stress hormone) and increased immunoglobulins (improved immunity)

Increased mindfulness: As one gets more "still" through practicing conscious breathing, they also become more aware of their thoughts and feelings. Once this happens, over time you will learn to choose which ones serve you and which ones don't, how to appreciate a moment and how to help yourself through a difficult one.

Practice:

Get into a comfortable position on a supportive piece of furniture. Ensure there are no external interruptions; phones are turned off, and there is complete peace and quiet. Put your hands on your lap, palms up.

Close your eyes and relax. Then focus on your breath as you inhale through your nose and exhale through your mouth. Breathe naturally and don't try to artificially increase the length of exhalation and inhalation. Do this for five minutes.

If thoughts begin to enter your mind, refocus on your breathing. If thoughts persist, try focusing on something else, like all the sounds you can hear. Don't try to analyze them; remember them and just experience them. This is not a test of memory; it's an exercise in mindfulness.

If you find it difficult to focus on your breath, think of an activity that brings you peace or joy or a release of stress. After you have done this, observe what activity came up for you that provided relief or joy. Journal or record your observations.

2.   Open Monitoring

Once you have been able to achieve focused attention you are now ready for Open Monitoring during which you have no object of focus but rather expand your vision and remain non-judgmentally receptive to any physical and mental phenomena that arise.

The practice of presence or mindfulness should not be confined just to your comfortable sofa a few minutes a day. With practice that mindset can be brought into different situations in your everyday life and through neuroplasticity you will be able to more effectively manage your emotions and your thoughts.

Practice:

Stop reading for a moment, look away from your screen or book and expand your gaze. Observe for a moment the entirety of your surroundings. Where are you now? How does it feel being here? Don't criticize your thoughts or feelings just be aware of them.

Next time you're out for a walk or in a busy mall or workspace, do the same, just observe what you are witnessing and feeling without judgment.

Repeat this practice as often as you remember it, journal what you experience each time you do it. Do you notice things you once wouldn't have? Do you feel your feelings shifting several times with each passing thought?

3.   Transcend Old Ways of Being

Self-Awareness, Regulation and Transcendence (S-ART)

Vago and Silversweig comment...

"The S-ART framework operates using the underlying premise that our perception, cognitions, and emotions related to our ordinary experiences can be distorted or biased to varying degrees. Depending on certain dispositional factors, these biases are sometimes pathological, but exist on a spectrum and may therefore be present without any clear psychopathology. Within this framework, mindfulness is described to reduce such biases through specific forms of mental training that develop meta-awareness of self (self-awareness), an ability to effectively manage or alter one's responses and impulses (self-regulation), and the development of a positive relationship between self and other that transcends self-focused needs and increases prosocial characteristics (self-transcendence)."

References

Rhonda Byrne (2007) *The Secret.* Atria Books

Lisa Barrett (2017) *How Emotions Are Made: The Secret Life of the Brain.* Mariner.

Ferriss, Tim (2009) *The 4-Hour Workweek, Expanded and Updated: Expanded and Updated, With Over 100 New Pages of Cutting-Edge Content.* Harmony

Frankl, V. (1946) *Man's Search for Meaning.*

Earl Nightingale (1956) *The Strangest Secret*

Grant Renier and Howard Rankin (2021) *Intuitive Rationality: The New Behavioral Approach to AI.*

Michael Singer (2015) *The Surrender Experiment: My Journey into Life's Perfection.* Harmony/Rodale

Nassim Taleb. (2014) *Antifragile: Things That Gain from Disorder.* Random House

Vago, D and Silberzweig (2012) Self-awareness, self-regulation, and self-transcendence (S-ART): a framework for understanding the neurobiological mechanisms of mindfulness. Front. Hum. Neurosci., 25 October 2012.

Varela, F. J., Thompson, E., and Rosch, E. (1991). *The Embodied Mind.* Cambridge, MA: MIT Press.

Chapter 4

Purpose

*"To be nobody but yourself in a world which is doing its best,
night and day, to make you everybody else means to fight the
hardest battle which any human being can fight; and never stop
fighting."*
-E. E. Cummings

Contributors: Ann Boothello, Angela Faye, Paola Hurtado,
Eric Patel

Purpose is a word that has different meanings. There is the overarching view of purpose referring to your inner purpose: your goal and your intended legacy. It's your statement of who you aspire to be.

Another meaning of the word relates to strategy: what's the goal of this particular action? This refers to an actionable purpose: What's the point of this action?

Inner purpose refers to the overall goal while actionable purpose is about the actions needed to manifest that goal. It is connected to human essence: who you are and the meaning of your life. It's the foundation to live a meaningful life. Purpose is not about who you are or who you want to be. It is about the legacy you want to leave in the world. It is the thing you bring to the table that disappears if you do not show up.

Inner purpose is linked to your values, but it is more than the sum of your values. It's linked to passion and curiosity and moves us to action. Passion is one thing that keeps recurring in our thinking and experiences. Inner purpose can be an engine for continuity and evolution. Creating meaning from events and actions over time shapes your impact on the world.

Inner purpose is connected to focus. Without inner purpose we cannot navigate today's world full of change. It gives us clarity, helps us to make choices and gives us meaning. Inner purpose makes us freer and gives us confidence to act.

Massive Transformative Purpose (MTP)

Massive Transformative Purpose (MTP) is a long-term statement of how we would like to see the world some 30 years from now.

- Self-awareness is the first step: connect with yourself, who you really are, what your values and motivations are and what you bring to the table.
- Shaping the world you want to impact is the second step. How do you leverage who you are and service society?
- The third step is connected to your legacy, the interaction between your inside and the outside. The outcome of that is to transform the world into a better place. This gives meaning to our lives and contributes to our happiness.

Big Hairy Audacious Goals (BHAGs)

BHAGs are long-term goals guided by your core values and inner purpose/MTP. BHAGs get you out of thinking too small and into thinking big.

Out of the four broad categories of BHAGs the two that are most applicable to individuals are:

- Role model: seek to emulate the results of a successful person.
- Internal transformation: remain competitive/relevant by revitalizing yourself.

The following checklist can be used when reviewing your BHAGs:

- Feels as if it's at least 70% achievable.
- Has to be clear and compelling.
- Expands your current capabilities (e.g., is a large stretch goal)
- Is measurable.
- Is long-term (10 - 25 years)

Moonshots

Moonshots are also long-term goals (e.g., 10 - 20 years into the future) that smash existing paradigms. A moonshot openly defies the majority opinion. All ground rules are subject to be changed. They are wild and free-range entities. They require throwing off the encumbrances of conventional, incremental thinking to achieve wholesale, exponential change.

The following skills will help you achieve your moonshots:

- Imagination
- Perception
- Curiosity
- Lateral thinking

Moonshots are connected to inner purpose. They make your inner purpose concrete. It is a way to quantify/measure your progress towards your purpose. Moonshots should be ambitious but ultimately achievable.

Ikigai

Ikigai can describe having a sense of purpose in life as well as being motivated. According to a study by Michiko Kumano, feeling ikigai as described in Japanese usually means the feeling of accomplishment and fulfillment that follows when people pursue their passions. Activities that generate the feeling of ikigai are not forced on an individual; they are perceived as being spontaneous and undertaken willingly and thus are personal and depend on a person's inner self.

According to ikigaitribe.com:

"Ikigai is not a term from Okinawa. It's not the Japanese secret to longevity. It's not a Venn diagram showing you how to find your bliss or become a successful entrepreneur. And it's not the pursuit of a single life purpose. It's a concept relatable to eudaemonia and existential positive psychology, ikigai offers you a way to guide others to live with motivation and resilience in times of hardship, opening them up to the path of self-actualization."

Ikigai is at the intersection of four concentric circles:

- What you're good at
- What you love
- What you can be paid for
- What the world needs

Each two circles also intersect to identify:

- Your passion: what you love + what you're good at
- Your profession: what you're good at + what you can be paid for
- Your mission: what you love + what the world needs
- Your vocation: what you can be paid for + what the world needs.

IKIGAI

A Japanese concept meaning 'a reason for being'

In keeping with the move from I to We, from Ego to We Go, we suggest renaming "I"kigai "we"kigai![1]

Virtues and Values

Virtues are personal traits, qualities or behavior exemplifying moral standards. The VIA Institute on Character has a complementary Strengths Profile that you can take. After answering a number of questions you'll receive your top virtues.

Values refer to beliefs or principles that guide our actions, attitudes and behavior. They are the core concepts or ideas that we consider important in our lives and help us to make decisions and judgments about what is right or wrong, good or bad, desirable or undesirable. Values are easy to identify: the hard part is living by them in challenging situations that we have not even experienced before.

Committing To Your Future Self

Later in this playbook you will formulate what your future self looks like (after baselining your current self). Your future self is who you aspire to become. Your journey is how you are going to get there. Becoming perfect is never the goal. You will strive to become the best version of yourself through self-awareness and human optimization, the core tenets of being an Exponential Individual.

Case study

In his book Why Do We Do It? Israeli American Moti Kahana outlines the key events in his life that made him a humanitarian who has given away his entire fortune and spent many years, often in risky conditions, trying to help others. Dr. Howard Rankin, a co-author of Kahana's book, outlines the details of a life that led to exponentiality.

Moti was the oldest of three boys and always had a sense of responsibility for his younger brothers, especially since they were brought up under very difficult conditions. Moti's father died when he was young and when his mother remarried a Druse man, Moti suffered a lot of abuse. He eventually ran away from home, was caught and subsequently sent into foster homes where abuse was also common. He was ultimately removed from these abusive environments. Whenever Moti was helped, he felt gratitude rather than anger. He could have easily joined criminal factions but he didn't. Instead, he felt responsibility and gratitude. He had also seen the ugly side of life and knew how many were suffering. These characteristics combined to make him a sensitive person who wanted to help others. He knew what it was like to suffer. He felt a responsibility to make a difference in the lives of others.

Moti was a successful businessman who gave his money to help the people of Syria after the Arab Spring uprising. He helped rebuild schools, rescued Jewish artifacts and helped many to escape the cruelty of war. He even managed to persuade doctors to provide medical care in Israeli hospitals for Syrian women and children in desperate need of healthcare. Subsequently, he helped people escape from Afghanistan and provided support and relief for Ukraine. Several times he even risked his life to help others escape the horrors of war.

Responsibility, gratitude, first-hand experience and emotional connection to those in need turned Moti into an exponential individual.

Finding your purpose and leveraging it to create a meaningful legacy begins by changing the way you think. You have to identify and remove habitual perceptions, cultural editors and social influences to find your own truth so you can manifest it as a meaningful contribution.

"All conditioned things are impermanent—when one sees this with wisdom, one turns away from suffering." -- Buddha

Exercises

1. Reflect in your journal what you believe the meaning of life is.
    a. Why am I here?
    b. Why do I think I'm here?
    c. What have I been put on earth for?

2. Describe your views on life and work.

3. Lifeline exercise: Create a timeline from your early childhood to the present time. The line should include peaks, valleys, plateaus and whatever else you want to include. The intensity of the situation or event can be illustrated by the height of the peak or depth of the valley. Feel free to get creative with different types of landmarks, colors and pictures. Identify the 3 best events and the 3 worst ones. Reflect about how you felt and why.

4. Reflect on your passions
   a. What is/are your passion/s?
   b. Describe a particular moment when you were fully experiencing your passion. Identify other moments like that one. How did you feel in those moments? Who were you in those moments?

5. What are the activities and interests that have stayed with you over time?

6. What makes you smile the most? Write down the words that are connected to that smile.

7. Journaling Your Ideal Day

What you want for your life really is possible. All of it. In order for you to effectively identify the internal conflicts that are preventing you from having it all, it's important for you to get clear on what your ideal day would look like. Most people don't have the clarity they need in order to chart an effective course to create their best life. In this exercise you can go through a short visualization process to get you imagining your Perfect 10 day. After the visualization we invite you to write down everything that you experienced in the space below. Even as you're journaling what you visualized you may have even more ideas come to your mind. You're welcome to write down those ideas as well.

8. Identify your role models/wisdom squad

9. Create one or more BHAGs congruent with your inner purpose

10. Create one or more moonshots congruent with your inner purpose

11. Take the VIA Character Strengths Profile and discover your top virtues

12. Create your Ikigai by answering these four questions:
    1. What are you good at?
    2. What do you love?
    3. What can you be paid for?
    4. What does the world need?

References

[1]Claudio Dipolitto, Brazil

Jim Collins and Jerry Porrs (2011) *Built to Last: Successful Habits of Visionary Companies.* Harper Business.

Rajeev Jain, and John Schroeter. (2018) *Moonshots: Creating a World of Abundance.* Moonshot Press

Links

Lifeline exercise
http://www.catalystleadershipcoaching.com/wp-content/uploads/2009/07/Lifeline-Exercise1.pdf

Earl Nightingale (2013). *The Strangest Secret.* Merchant Books https://www.youtube.com/watch?v=NbBHR_CD56M

Tim Ferriss Fear-Setting Exercise
https://tim.blog/2017/05/15/fear-setting/
https://www.teamstrength.com/wp-content/uploads/2018/03/Fear-Setting-with-Tim-Ferriss.pdf
https://www.amazon.com/Massive-Transformative-Purpose-provide-projects-ebook/dp/B09GY9BKVT

Mindsets and Moonshots - Peter Diamandis - MTP
https://franciscopalao.com/tools/mtp-canvas
https://github.com/exoeconomy/ExO-Tool-Kit/releases

Joe Dispenza (2013) Breaking the habit of being yourself. Hay House
https://www.youtube.com/watch?v=oFB6KDftGPY   ;
https://www.youtube.com/watch?v=z2EnsLBkiOQ

Business Model You: https://businessmodelyou.com/

Bill Burnett and Dav Evans. *Design Your Life:* (2016). Knopf.
https://www.amazon.com/dp/B01BJSRSEC/ref=dp-kindle-redirect?_encoding=UTF8&btkr=1

VIA Institute Character Test https://www.viacharacter.org

Chapter 5

Where Are You?

"Yesterday I was clever, so I wanted to change the world. Today I am wise, so I am changing myself."
- *Rumi*

<u>Contributors</u>: Kevin Allen, Mac Carvalho, Danielle Alice Desanges Auceane Thiam Meka de Goguenheim, Dolapo Tukuru

This part of the playbook focuses on where you currently are in your life. Where you are now does not determine where your future will be. However, starting on this journey requires an understanding of where you are now.

In order to understand your decision-making and life circumstances it is important to assess your current status in multiple pillars of life. These pillars are:

- Health and Wellness
- Beliefs and Emotions
- Work and Career
- Money and Finance
- Learning and Growth
- Friends and Community
- Family and Love
- Spirituality and Purpose

This evaluation is key to a better understanding of yourself and how to release your full potential. As you conduct this evaluation, be honest about where you are now in each of these pillars and the importance of each in your life now and in the future.

Health and Wellness

- How much of a priority is your health and wellness?
- How much of a priority would you want it to be in the future?
- Do you get regular medical check-ups?
- Do you seek information about health and wellness?
- Do you engage in regular exercise?
- Do you manage your weight effectively?
- Do you sleep well?
- Do you eat healthy?
- Do you get enough rest and relaxation?
- Do you manage stress effectively?

Beliefs and Emotions

- What are your core beliefs about life in general?
- What are your core beliefs about yourself?
- Where do these beliefs come from?
- Have you ever changed previously strongly held beliefs?
- How good are you at managing your emotions?
- What specific techniques do you use to manage your emotions?
- What triggers you to get upset or angry?
- Do you consider yourself open-minded?

Work and Career

- What are the core components of a good work life for you?
- How satisfying is your work life?
- Is your work stimulating and challenging?
- Is your work overwhelming or stressful?
- Have you thought about changing your career?
- Do you feel you have control over your work life?
- How could your current work situation be improved?
- Do you have a vision for your future work life?
- Do you explore other opportunities that might interest you?

Money and Finance

- Do you have a well-articulated and long-term financial plan?
- Do you regularly put money aside into savings, investments and/or retirement?
- Do you have a budget or set limits on your spending?
- How much debt do you have?
- Do you live paycheck-to-paycheck, month-to-month?
- Do you know your total monthly expenses?
- Would you like to be a better money manager?
- Do you have a professional financial advisor?

Learning and Growth

- Do you take courses on subjects that interest you?
- Is learning important to you?
- What subjects do you want to know more about?
- Do you ever go to talks and presentations?

- Do you think that you have learned all you need to know?
- Do you believe that learning could enhance your life?
- If you had the time, what courses or classes would you like to take?
- How many books do you read or audiobooks do you listen to each month?
- Do you prefer fiction or non-fiction books?

Friends and Community

- Do you have a good circle of friends?
- Are you involved in any community activities?
- Do you volunteer for any causes?
- How important are relationships for you?
- How often do you get together with friends?
- How important is your social life?
- Would you like to improve your connections with friends and the community?
- Do you belong to any groups?

Family and Love

- How important are family connections for you?
- Are you satisfied with your current connections with family members?
- How could relationships with family members be improved?
- Do you feel loved?
- Do you think you could be more loving?
- How could you be more loving?
- Are you sharing your life with someone special?

Spirituality and Purpose

- How important is spirituality to you?
- What spiritual activities are you currently engaged in?
- Would you like to engage in more spiritual activities?
- Does the concept of spirituality appeal to you? Why?
- Do you feel you have purpose in your life?
- How aware of that purpose are you on a daily basis?
- Can you articulate what your purpose is?
- What do you want your legacy to be?
- What are your religious beliefs?

The Wheel of Life tool helps you assess your life in several areas: health, career, love, spirituality, family, money, fun and friends. See the link at the end of the chapter where you can take this assessment.

Human beings are meaning-makers and thus storytellers. We each have stories about who we are and those stories can be very influential in directing our thoughts, feelings and behaviors. We are programmed to find meaning and make connections between events often without any supporting information. Just because two events happen simultaneously they may not be related in any way. While this is most noticeable around public discourse it also can happen to us personally. We can misinterpret events and these thoughts can turn into misguided beliefs that shape our self-concept.

The story we tell ourselves powerfully impacts our self-image. It is a natural inclination to weave together our lives into stories. It is important to be aware of your story and change it if needed so it better serves you.

Exercises

1. What's your story? Who are you?

A proper evaluation of your current self requires that you are able to look at yourself from the outside. This requires an open mind and it is not easy. This is one of the reasons why many of us simply go through life as a victim of circumstance: we go along with cultural traditions, habits and perspectives, never appreciating that we can step outside these limits and see the world and ourselves much differently.

Self-awareness may seem like something that is pretentious, and we might be irritated by people that are self-aware and let us know how self-aware they are. But self-awareness isn't pretentious; it is essential if you want to understand the full range of your experiences and your possibilities.

> *"True behavior change is identity change."*
> *- James Clear, Atomic Habits*

Self-assessment

How many of your behaviors are blindly following norms attached to your identity?

To transform, focus on identity-based habits vs outcome-based habits. The former are behaviors that flow from and reinforce your perceived identity. Outcome-based habits are behaviors that flow from repetition of a behavior to achieve certain goals.

Imagine two people refusing a cigarette. When offered a smoke the first person says "No thanks. I'm trying to quit." It sounds like a reasonable response but this person believes they are a smoker who is trying to be something else. They are hoping their behavior will change while carrying the same belief.

The second person declines by saying, "No thanks. I'm not a smoker." It is a small difference but this statement signals a shift in identity. Smoking was part of their formal life, not their current one. They no longer identify as someone who smokes.

The starting point is being aware of how you self-identify.

Journal your recurring thoughts/self-identity statements or how others have labeled you. For example:

> "I'm always late."
> "I'm bad at remembering people's names."
> "I'm scared to share my opinions at work."
> "I should do more exercise."
> "I'm too nice."
> "I'm really good at…"

The biggest barrier to positive change at any level - individual, team, society - is identity conflict.

Good habits can make rational sense but if they conflict with your current identity, you will fail to put them into action effectively.

For example, you might go on a "diet" for a few days before old habits take over again.

New identities require new evidence. We do not achieve massive change simply by snapping our fingers. We change bit-by-bit, day-by-day, habit-by-habit. Every action you take is a vote for the type of person you wish to become.

Becoming exponential is a commitment to making greater impact with the same amount of input. For example:

- Every time you write a page you are a writer. Every time you choose to share your voice/learning/insights with others you are becoming exponential.

- Each time you encourage your employees/audience you are a leader. If you share your encouragement or contribution with a bigger audience, you are becoming exponential.

The next step is a realignment to who you want to be.

The Self Awareness Map

If we think of life as a journey, knowing where you are can be related to location on a map. Designing a map of all the steps that one followed to be in one's present location can be very insightful, and you can also use the same concept to create the route for your next steps and even your ultimate destination. This can be applied to any area of life: spiritual, emotional, professional or intellectual. A map is a synthesis of information or metadata around a subject that helps visually create a sense of localization to put space and time into perspective.

One helpful metaphor is to think of our life's journey as a pathway paved with stones. When we look backwards into our past steps it is possible to identify stages or states, when and where we were successful or not. Each stage would be represented by a stone of a different color or texture. In that way we can figure out patterns of success and failure and learn from those patterns. Moving forward, our challenge would be to find the right path or the right stones to step on based on our learnings.

The whole path of stones, where and when we felt better, happy, in flow or any other expression of completeness, is what we call the purpose of life. Having an inner purpose is to understand and uncover this pathway and being able to live by purpose is to acknowledge the best stones to step on and build a path forward.

Another way to look at this is to use natural processes as a model in an effort not to create more artificial ways to describe who we are. Exponentiation is natural: it is present in nature's processes. For instance, the way a virus spreads shows us how natural systems can adapt and find their way through life to maintain its "life purpose." In the virus example, it wants to survive, to preserve itself and not disappear. So it may seem unnecessary when we think of an "exponential" individual. It might sound redundant because by nature everyone has exponential growth patterns inside but often the perception of the outer world limits those possibilities. Awakening the Exponential Individual within is to make the self-awareness map clearer, increase its definition and its resolution. If only we could look inside using the eyes of the soul the resolution of that image would be an infinite number of pixels per inch.

Looking at humanity's history we can see several information structures that helped ancient people to map their journey. For example, religious books help to identify the values and principles of a population or group of people. They became a map of the information around social behavior and relationships. This design can be modeled using the latest technologies to create a broader expression on how to present the purpose or the "self-awareness map".

Links

https://wheeloflife.noomii.com

Chapter 6

Who Do You Want to Become?

"Our prime purpose in this life is to help others.
And if you can't help them, at least don't hurt them."
– Dalai Lama

<u>Contributors</u>: Kevin Allen, Anthony Boschi, David Forman, Paola Hurtado, Mynor Schultz, Howard Rankin

Now that you've defined where you are at, it's time to look at where you're going. This chapter contains several exercises that will help you define and visualize the person you want to become. So, get out a blank notepad, and fill it up with thoughts and ideas as you read along.

Imagine Your Future Life

Imagine your life ten years from now. Visualize your greatest possibilities. Try to make it the most vivid, fulfilled life possible. What does your day look like? How are you spending your time? Who are you surrounding yourself with?

Visualization is a powerful tool. It is real practice that can begin to create changes in the brain that underpin new behaviors which is why many athletes use it. There are many examples of how visualization can be effective.

In one study at Ohio University in 2014, two sets of study participants had one of their wrists immobilized by putting it in a cast for four weeks. One group was instructed to sit still and "intensely imagine exercising for 11 minutes, five days a week." They were told to put all their energy into this visualization task. The other group were not told to visualize or given any specific instructions. At the end of the four weeks the visualizers had twice the strength than the other group in their wrists. Moreover, neuroimaging showed that the visualizers had created changes in their brains consistent with increased strength in their immobilized wrists.

In another famous example a US soldier Major James Nesmeth was held captive in a small cage by the Vietcong for several years. After the first few weeks he knew he had to escape mentally if he was to survive. He was an avid golfer with a 22 handicap and generally shot around 94. He decided that he would spend as much time as he could each day visualizing playing a successful round of golf at his local club.

With time to kill, he became very detailed in his visualizations. He visualized what he was wearing, who he was playing with, the weather conditions, the blades of grass, everything he could imagine. He visualized the trajectory of every shot and where and how it landed. It took him as much time to visualize playing a round as it did actually playing a round.

He did this for seven years. He was finally released, a very fragile figure and nothing like the strong and fit man who was captured. A few days after he arrived home, he decided he wanted to play on his home golf course. He drove out to the golf course not sure what to expect. He shot a 74, his best round ever. Don't be surprised: he had been practicing every day for seven years!

Like the soldier in the story above, the more specific you can be, the better. What you visualize, you are practicing. You are activating and building the neural pathways that ultimately will be the infrastructure of your new behavior.

Try to imagine all of the particular details that make your life feel outstanding. Try not to compare this vision to your current life and limitations but instead imagine the greatest possibilities in the greatest detail.

Repeat this exercise for the end of your life: imagine you are on your deathbed looking back at the incredible journey of your lifetime. How do you feel? What kind of relationships do you want to have? What kind of impact do you want to have during your lifetime? What parts of your life are the most important? What is your legacy?

Once we've identified what is important to us we can reverse-engineer what it means to lead a well-lived life in accordance with our values. We also have a baseline, a litmus, with which we can at any time measure or evaluate alignment or lack thereof, as well as morph and change our aspirations which are usually never static.

Imagine that you could design your own superhero who is the best version of you in the future. What qualities would they have and portray? In what way could you embody this design? Write down a number of qualities. Trust yourself and know you are capable and worthy.

As a final exercise imagine if you were born in a different time and place: imagine being born as someone else, some other gender, ethnicity, upbringing or a different person entirely. What would it be like?

Being your true self is an act of love. Seek out the ways by which you can express yourself and give yourself permission to play in the playground of life itself. While doing so, look to retrospectively determine when you were so entranced by a passion that you feel you had merged your action and awareness: where your sense of self was not just in the mind but also in the heart and the environment. This is flow and this may be your calling.

The act of wanting to be is a reflection of an in-the-moment feeling. There is an interesting dynamic between having a conviction for what you desire and simultaneously letting life unfold as it's meant to. So how do we achieve a future self when we don't even know what the future holds? One way is to be aware of the preconceived notions that you may have about what this future self would do for your sense of belonging in the world. This allows you to tackle the psychological barriers of not feeling worthy in the present that may be holding you back.

Inner Purpose, Vision and Mission statements

Once you have identified your pure reasons for this idea of future self you can direct your attention to what this future self does in service to others: this is the materialization of the Massive Transformative Purpose.

If you create your inner purpose based on a dysfunctional belief it will be unlikely that you are going to achieve it. An example of dysfunctional belief is, "I do not understand how things work at my job. It's all about office politics". Reframing this dysfunctional belief results in a new idea: "I can learn how to succeed by learning how I manage influence, authority and power."

Once you have created your inner purpose let's reimagine how we can design our vision and mission statements. Perhaps we view these from the vantage point of our already-envisioned future and reverse engineer the process.

For our vision statement we can take a look at what our ideal day looks like. Expecting the ideal to crystallize in the way we perceive is the fallacy, so this gives us a space to be playful and imaginative with the experiment.

With self-awareness being at the forefront of any introspective process it is important to acknowledge a level of openness in one's intentions and the occurrences of life since we are not expansive enough to account for everything, that is, for the intelligence of life itself.

Thinking about this ideal day you can imagine the scope of your experience and all that it may entail that illustrates what you truly intend to focus on in this forecasted phase of your life (you can have many "ideal days"). It can be perceived through scenarios, words, emotions and whichever medium of interpretation that activates your internal senses that ignite deep feelings of passion and ease. The culmination of this iterative process will bring about an insight, a rhythm of what your vision is, distilled into the experiences that we categorize into days. Therein lies your vision statement in whatever form it may take.

As for your mission statement you can think of this as your why: why are you seeking the vision and what would you like to achieve, contribute and serve?

For this process you can apply the same reverse engineering principles and attempt to imagine the experience that will emerge as a result of your focus and action. These experiences are through the lens of what others will gain as the consequence of your actions. Do you see their life enhanced? In what ways could they take these goals that you have contributed to and expand them in their own rite? Your 'why' becomes bigger than just you and what you want: it is a human serving humanity.

To get a clearer idea of your why, it can be very helpful to acknowledge the feeling you are trying to elicit within yourself. Oftentimes we seek to quench an internal ideal (whether we are aware of it or not) and then marvel at the thought that it could benefit others as if it were simply a collateral effect and not the actual mission. So how can we make sure that the mission statement is there really for the mission itself? By learning to satisfy your own needs without external changes. By taking note of what elicits visceral emotions by way of reaction. Do you know why the emotions you experience arise? Maybe you are looking for respect, attention or praise which aren't being met in the expectations of your environment. When you clear the fog of what you are truly after and articulate them to yourself, your mission for others will be an inherent intention of the soul and not just the mind. Therefore, even greater connection can be developed with others which exceeds that of what you were initially attempting to satisfy within yourself. This is where your "why" can fly free, where you can merge your vision and mission statements.

Exercises

1. Use the self-awareness map to determine where you want to go and how you are going to get there.
2. Revisit the Ikigai image in chapter 4 and make any needed updates
3. Write your eulogy. How do you want to be remembered?

References

Clark BC, Mahato NK, Nakazawa M, Law TD, Thomas JS. (2014) *The Power of the Mind: The Cortex as a Critical Determinant of Muscle Strength/Weakness.* J Neurophysiol. 2014 Dec 15;112(12):3219-26. doi: 10.1152/jn.00386.2014. Epub 2014 Oct 1. PMID: 25274345; PMCID: PMC4269707.

Chapter 7

Why Do People Really Change?

"Progress is impossible without change, and those who cannot change their minds cannot change anything."
- *George Bernard Shaw*

Contributors: Howard Rankin

In this playbook we give you tools to help you make the changes in your life that contribute to your exponential growth. Tools are important as they enable you to manifest your dreams by building new behaviors. They are necessary but not sufficient to transform your life. You need something else.

Did you hear about the gang member who became a rabbi? Or the voice of an anti-hate group who was twice imprisoned for hate crimes becoming one of the leading Catholic writers of his generation? Meet Joseph Pearce.

As per Wikipedia:

"At 15 Pearce joined the youth wing of the National Front (NF), an anti-Semitic and white supremacist political party advocating the compulsory repatriation of all immigrants and British-born non-whites. He came to prominence in 1977 when he set up Bulldog, the NF's openly-racist newspaper. Like his father, Pearce became an enthusiastic supporter of Ulster Loyalism during the Troubles from 1978, and joined the Orange Order, a militantly anti-Catholic secret society closely linked to Ulster Loyalist paramilitary organizations. In 1980 he became editor of Nationalism Today, advocating white supremacy. Pearce was twice prosecuted and imprisoned under the Race Relations Act of 1976 for his writings in 1981 and 1985."

It was while in prison for a second time that Pearce read G.K. Chesterton and eventually disavowed his previous views and became Catholic, the very identity he had been targeting with hate throughout his young life. He went on to become a prolific and heralded writer of many Catholic books.

Why then do people change? They can change when they are confronted by the inherent damage of their thinking and behavioral habits. And there's nothing more habitual than our thinking. We build our ideologies about the world and ourselves and habitually, often automatically, support and reinforce them at every opportunity, literally carving them into our brains by reinforcing the neural pathways that support our views. We literally are brain-washed and we do the washing or at the very least, allow it. We thus built a wall to protect our treasured beliefs.

So, what brings this wall crashing down? What changes a purveyor of hate into a devout Catholic?

Confrontation.

When denial no longer works, when rationalization dissolves and the wall is down, the mind is now open to anything and what especially attracts attention are the dialectic opposites to the very habitual thoughts and behaviors you have been relying on for your identity. That's when you hit rock bottom: when those notions and beliefs are smashed into pieces as they hit those rocks at the bottom.

Luckily many of us don't have to confront extremely hateful actions but we all have regrets. We all have done things we wished we hadn't, and we all have had various ideas and beliefs that have held us back. Some people don't have the courage to look there and continue to rationalize away, some do but don't believe they can do anything about it and some people just cry.

"God lets you hit rock bottom so you can discover
He is the rock at the bottom."
– Tony Evans

Imagine you are sitting outside with a friend. You look at the sky and then proclaim with some joy:

"Look at those clouds, they look just like an elephant!"

Your friend looks up and notices the similarity.

"Wow, you're so creative!" she says.

Actually, the clouds were like that for a few seconds. You didn't make the clouds look like an elephant; you just noticed it.

Perception is noticing what already exists and seeing it clearly. It's suspending the usual editors and lenses and seeing with clarity what is already there.

There once was a man sitting under a tree. He was watching sun rays filter through the clouds, creating an escalator of light that stretched from the sky to the fields below. The man had a thought.

"I wonder what it would be like to ride on a sunbeam?" he asked himself.

That man was Albert Einstein and his thought was the beginning of his Theory of Relativity.

"Imagination is more important than knowledge. For knowledge is limited, whereas imagination embraces the entire world, stimulating progress, giving birth to evolution."
– Albert Einstein

Notice his words: imagination embraces the entire world. It doesn't invent it, it embraces it. Some people will have an idea and assume that they own it and have created it. No, it was there waiting to be discovered and no doubt many others, maybe across the entire history of mankind, saw something similar but for whatever reason didn't do anything about it or did but no one knows about it.

One of the thinking habits and cognitive biases we use to keep us blind to change is called temporal discounting, the tendency to minimize the future and live in the present. As you will see, connection with your future self is critical. Without that connection you will be prevented from seeing the future consequences of your behavior.

One example could be smokers who justify their habit on the basis that their lung cancer is a long way off, and probably won't even happen. So, here's an exercise for smokers.

First, read this scene then imagine it as vividly as possible.

"There's a man being hurriedly taken off an ambulance and is being carried through the emergency room. He is pale and almost in a coma and is connected to a machine that is keeping him alive. Just behind the stretcher are three people. They are distraught and crying even as they are trying to keep up with the stretcher that is being pulled at emergency speed. You are that dying man. They are your loved ones, desperately hoping these aren't your last moments, the last seconds spent with a husband and a father. Put yourself on that stretcher. Your lungs are failing. You need a machine to breathe, to stay alive. Do you want a cigarette? Or do you try to bargain with your God: save me and I promise I'll never smoke another cigarette again?"

There are many people who have made that promise not just to their God but to their amazing mind-body-spirits. Now aligned with their mind-body-spirit to restore and preserve health, many of those people have made incredible, often miraculous recoveries. They have had their eyes opened and embraced an alternative truth that has been there all along.

Let's consider a different example.

A woman, let's call her Eve, has a mother who has dementia but insists on living at home. Eve's two other siblings take turns to be with her mother and take care of her. They travel to her home and spend weeks of their time, making sure their mother is comfortable, giving her meds and giving the care and love she desperately needs. But Eve doesn't want to do that. She thinks her mother can be very difficult and doesn't do what she is told. Eve would have to rearrange her life to spend time with a very difficult person and her two siblings can cope much better with this than she can. Eve does nothing and lets her siblings do all the work. Moreover, she expects to get her share of her mother's estate when she dies.

What happens when Eve's mother dies? Does she feel guilty? Does she continue to justify her behavior? Does the antagonism between her and her siblings continue? Or does she have regrets?

Let's suppose Eve had opened her eyes instead of defending herself and hiding behind her wall. The moral issue here is not about whether to contribute to her dying mother's care but how to contribute. Morality and virtue suggest she has to make a contribution; there's no choice about that.

Instead of being antagonistic towards her siblings Eve might have said: "Even though I have a tough time being with mom, in what other ways could I contribute?"

Perhaps she could help financially, spend a few days with mom to give her siblings a break, finance a caregiver for a few days to give her siblings a break or volunteer to take over some of the administrative details of mom's life such as legal and financial matters.

The answer is always rooted in values and virtues. When you are led by anything else you are avoiding the issue, and not seeing the real possibilities. Look at nature. Look into your mind-body-spirit. The answer is there.

Why do people struggle with change? Because they discount the future, close their eyes to possibilities, defend their ideologies and build a wall behind which to hide.

Studies in cultural neuroscience show how much culture can change not just our thinking but also our brains.

In an article in the Association for Psychological Science neuroscientist and researcher Nalini Ambady writes:

"Solving basic arithmetic problems activates the Broca's and Wernicke's brain areas, the main parts of the brain also involved in the processing of language. However, in a 2006 study comparing native Chinese and native English speakers solving these same simple math problems, Tang and colleagues discovered that among native Chinese speakers, there was not only less activation in these language-related areas than among the English speakers, but also more activation in the premotor cortex areas associated with movement. These researchers suggested that the source of this difference might be the Chinese language's focus on images and writing in contrast to the sound-focused English language in which each letter has a particular sound. Thus, areas associated with vision and movement might be more useful in accessing the rules for solving a math problem for Chinese speakers, whereas areas linked to language processing and verbal information might be more involved for English speakers' solution of the same problem.

So although Chinese and Americans alike should arrive at the same conclusion that $2 + 2 = 4$, the internal paths they navigate to get there seem to be quite different."

Not only are there differences in the neurological mechanisms used to solve problems but different cultures also sometimes use the same brain mechanisms to reach different conclusions. For example, in evaluating political candidates both American and Japanese participants used the amygdala – the part of the brain engaged in the processing of emotions – to make their decisions. However, the Americans were looking for signs of strength and power while the Japanese were looking for empathy, warmth and compassion.

Our thinking is massively influenced by both our macro and micro cultures. At the macro level are the societal expectations and definitions of success as well as our language, heritage, ethnicity and customs. At the micro level we are massively influenced by our upbringing, home life, family and early experience. All of these manipulate the brain to go down very specific paths which we almost never challenge. However, there are many other alternatives to our ideas that come from these thinking habits.

The secret to wisdom and exponential development is the ability to see these habitual editors and the influences that generated them. And having gained awareness of these limitations, look beyond them and be open to different alternatives.

Courage is casting off the usual defenses and being willing to see the possibilities that are there to be seen. You just have to open your eyes to see them.

Exercises

1. What rationalizations are holding you back from being exponential?
2. To what extent do you base your desires and goals on virtues and values?
3. How do you stay open to possibilities?
4. What thoughts come to mind when you think about your future self?
5. What habits would you like to change? What would your new habits be?

References

Nalini Ambady (2011) *The Mind in the World: Culture and the Brain. Association for Psychological Science,* May 4, 2011. https://www.psychologicalscience.org/observer/the-mind-in-the-world-culture-and-the-brain

Chapter 8

How to Get There

"Success is a journey, not a destination.
The doing is often more important than the outcome."
– Arthur Ashe

Contributors: David Forman, Steven Rodriguez, Mynor Schultz,

Now that you've articulated who you are and who you want to become, we can now figure out how to get you there.

If this seems daunting don't worry. One approach we can take is to reverse-engineer the process. Ask yourself: What do I want to do next month, next year and beyond and work backwards from that.

Without honest clarity regarding how an individual truly wants to live their life it's challenging to create worthwhile goals, Objectives and Key Results (OKRs) and Key Performance Indicators (KPIs). Hopefully you have done that through the previous chapters. If you still are unclear of your inner purpose some of these tools will help you articulate what you really want.

Many of us still don't know what we want to do with our lives but we can use tools such as the iKigai map to gauge where your interest and natural abilities lie. Once you do that you can take steps towards things you are curious to learn more about. You may be curious about exponential technologies or planetary consciousness in which case you can ask yourself, "What do I want to experience or learn about it?" and then take a step. To structure this thought process, list all the things that interest you and discover what you feel about them, experiment and learn.

SMART Goals

There's a saying that in order to get to where we want to go we will need to know where we're going. There's usually a lot going on in our lives and we can easily get distracted and derailed. To minimize distractions and stay focused, having a system to manage our daily output is what seems to work best for most people.

You can use a technique called writing SMART goals to help you reach your outcomes more effectively.

We can write out goals, so they reflect the following criteria: Specific, Measurable, Achievable, Realistic and Time-bound:

- Specific: Goals need to be well-defined: determine the who, what, where, when and why.
- Measurable: Develop criteria for measuring progress. Identify the key indicators that help you decide if and when you reach your goal by quantifying them.
- Achievable: Create goals that you'll be able to actually complete
- Realistic: Ensure goals are not out of reach by being too much of a stretch goal
- Time-bound: Create a deadline for reaching your goal to provide a sense of urgency and the opportunity to schedule the steps you plan to take in order to achieve the goal.

Successful goal achievement can be attributed to proper planning and executing against deliverables in a realistic amount of time to achieve the desired outcome.

Objectives and Key Results (OKRs)

One of the most fundamental and practical tools is the use of OKRs. They help define and obtain what an individual wants or needs to achieve and measure progress toward actionable purpose.

What's beneficial about OKRs is that they elicit and drive fundamental mindset changes especially in the areas of innovation, communication, and collaboration.

When OKRs are applied correctly they empower a person to show up every day with passion and purpose not just physically and mentally but also emotionally.

Once you have a clear understanding of your inner purpose and how it contributes to your life's mission, you'll be prepared to show up to do your best every day.

The identification of your what and why are necessary before effective goal setting can occur. The individual should have a well-defined life's mission in alignment with his/her own values. OKRs help exponential individuals to fulfill their mission by setting measurable objectives.

Real progress is most likely to occur when individuals are aligned and focused on achieving outcomes supporting a well-defined mission.

For example, Steve Jobs in his introduction to the famous Think Different advertising campaign clearly defined his new mission at Apple: to "enable passionate people to change the world." Reconnecting with their mission allowed Apple to recover from near-bankruptcy and irrelevance to becoming one of the world's most valuable brands.

A well-defined and emotionally-effective inner purpose coupled with moonshots and a well-understood mission are prerequisites to maximizing the effectiveness of OKRs.

Without an understanding of what exactly you are trying to achieve it will be challenging to reach your target, much less build a community of supporters or followers that could help you reach your goals. Individuals should be aligned with their inner purpose or with their soul. The individual's mission must live in his/her heart.

OKRs link goals and effort. One of the biggest challenges of setting OKRs is not understanding their purpose or relationship to other processes.

Let's start with what OKRs are not. An OKR is not a goal: the goal is what we ultimately want; the objective is something we accomplish in a given timeframe that supports the accomplishment of the goal. An OKR is not a KPI. It's not a task: a task is a specific work unit such as "Write a blog post how to write an OKR" or "Implement push notifications feature."

OKRs are also not meant to be a to-do list.

What then is an OKR? It is a framework used to set and measure goals and objectives. OKRs consist of two main components:

1. Objectives: These are the goals that you want to achieve. Objectives should be specific, measurable, achievable, relevant and time-bound (SMART)
2. Key Results: These are the metrics used to measure progress towards the objectives. Key results should be quantifiable and measurable.

OKRs help you |achieve the desired goal. We start with the goals that we want to achieve. From these goals, we derive the objectives that will have the desired impact on our goals when accomplished. Then we define key results which when met, will indicate we have completed our objective. Finally, we decide on how we will use our resources to accomplish our key results. Those are tasks.

Goals and objectives are not identical. A goal is a higher-level target we want to achieve. The objective is more refined and time bound.

For example, our personal goal could be to have a net worth of $1 million. There are many ways and strategies you could reach this goal and all those ways represent objectives. For example, investing in technology stocks could be one such objective. A task could be buying a specific stock.

How do I create an OKR?

The first thing one needs to decide is the goal one wants to achieve. The goal could be anything that you want to happen or not happen. Here are some examples:

- Increase your savings or net worth.
- Start your own business or graduate from college.
- Raise awareness of a specific problem.

Let's say that you want to learn how to become a life coach. This is a great personal goal and potentially your mastery of it could help many others.

Now that you know exactly the goal you want to work towards, it's time to pick a specific objective you believe will get you there. What you need to consider are some objectives that, when accomplished, will bring you closer to your goal. Defining these objectives is not simple so you need to do some critical and analytical thinking. The proper analysis yields tremendous results down the road.

Let's suppose that after some consideration you conclude that becoming a coach will elevate your exponential skills. Your objective for next quarter could be to research and learn more about the coaching profession. Therefore, we have the following:

Goal: Become a life coach
Objective: Research and learn more about the coaching profession

Time to set some key results.

What are you going to do to explore the coaching field in the next several weeks?

Consider and research possibilities. You come up with the following key results:

- Enroll in an online course.
- Read 3 books on coaching.
- Identify and speak with a coach about the profession and his or her experiences.

Now you have set three key results to achieve your objective.

Tips for Successful OKR Implementation

Unsuccessful OKR programs are characterized by minimal buy-in, leading to trying something new each quarter or even every month. Keep in mind that some of the first implementation attempts of OKR programs fail. Keep trying until it gains traction.

It's not recommended to rush any OKR implementation process since this could lead to failure. Even if the implementation is done correctly when the OKRs process is mismanaged it will suffer a setback. Adequate support of the OKR program is critical.

One needs to commit time, resources, attitude and responsibility to manage the process.

A properly written, managed and implemented OKR program entices other people to consider their own OKR program. Any individual can implement a successful OKR program without special tools, great expertise or tremendous insight. However, introducing and embedding an OKR practice within yourself may not be as easy.

Here are some tips to ensure that your OKR implementation is successful:

1. Implementing OKRs at first may seem intimidating. Stay on track and get constructive feedback.
2. You want to accomplish an objective within a given time frame which will have the desired effect on your goals.
3. Key results are indicators that show when you've reached your objective. Tasks are the jobs that you undertake to achieve your key results.
4. Putting effort into well-defined OKRs is important. As the adage says: "Measure twice, cut once."
5. OKRs are used for everything that the individual truly wants to accomplish, and this is the main reason they are one of the most effective tools for an Exponential Individual.

Case Study

As a community builder Shirley was usually involved with a business program or initiative. Techstars' Startup Weekend (SW) is a fun initiative to help the next generation of founders explore the highs and lows of trying to build a business from an idea. In the most recent one, Shirley decided to implement OKRs to more effectively reach her targets. Here's how she began to incorporate the process to improve outcomes.

One growing gap was the level of support that the participants received at critical times during the 54-hour bootcamp. Let's see how Shirley could begin to close the gap using OKRs:

Objective: Help SW volunteers guide and support participants better.
KR1: Develop an expanded orientation workshop to help volunteers better aid organizers and participants by February 28
KR2: Host 20 new volunteers for an expanded orientation around Startup Weekend support
KR3: Achieve a workshop(s) Net Promoter Score (NPS) of > 8.0
KR4: Maintain a 30-minute (maximum) response time in the guide support queue during SW

In order to improve the experience for volunteers and participants she decided to develop an orientation workshop to better train and equip the volunteers who assist participants during critical engagement moments during SW.

With the workshop agenda completed, Shirley decided to recruit a few people to experiment and learn. We needed to collect and assess NPS scores to see how the volunteers felt so she could improve it prior to the next cohort.

For the outcome to achieve her goal Shirley selected a response time key result (KR) to better assess if volunteers were adequately prepared and for answering questions.

Key Performance Indicators (KPIs)

A KPI is a measurable value that is used to track the performance of an organization, team or individual against specific goals and objectives. KPIs are used to monitor progress towards goals and to identify areas that need improvement or optimization.

The "K" stands for key, meaning what is truly important. The "P" stands for performance, what outcomes you are looking for. The "I" stands for indicator, a measurement to illustrate if you are lagging or leading toward your objectives.

OKRs set the path for the intention of those goals and KPIs show us if we are making progress toward those important goals. OKRs show us the tactical process to obtain or achieve our desired goals. KPIs measure our progress (or lack of) toward the specific actions required to achieve those goals.

We could have KPIs for anything that is important in our lives as KPIs allow us to measure our performance over time to obtain a specific strategic objective. Basically, KPI's allow us to judge the effectiveness of our efforts so we can make better decisions.

Let's say that one of your goals this year is to improve your health and fitness level. You decide to run the 26.2 miles needed to complete a marathon. The objective is to run a marathon and some of the key results could be to run a half marathon four months down the road and complete a 10k run in the next two months.

You discover that a good time to complete the marathon for your age group is in about five hours. What that means for you is that in six months when you run your first marathon you will need to run each mile at a pace of 11 minutes and 45 seconds.

To accomplish this goal, you need some KPIs to show you if you are moving towards your OKR. Effective KPIs help avoid unpleasant surprises on your marathon day. For example, on your first day of training you can hardly keep up with a 15-minute mile pace, way up from the target of 11:45. However, you still have 20 weeks ahead to train and reduce those times.

You decide that your KPIs to reach this OKR are going to be as follows:

- Week 1: no time measurement, just want to work into your schedule your daily running routine.
- Week 2: Run 3 miles comfortably at a 15-minute pace. (KPI = 15')
- Week 5: Run a couple of miles at a 14-minute pace. (KPI = 14')
- Week 10; Run at a 13-mile pace. (KPI = 13')
- Week 15: Run at a 12-mile pace. (KPI = 12')
- Week 20: Run at 11:50 mile pace. (KPI = 11:50')
- Week 24: Run at 11:45 mile pace. (KPI = 11:45')

Case study

Jim is in his late twenties. He has been focusing on increasing his wealth. After a baseline assessment, he realized that he had $15,000 in debt, no assets (e.g., home ownership, investments) and no plan to manage his finances. With some SMART goals, Jim came to the conclusion that he needed to get out of debt within two years. OKRs helped him chart a path on how to accomplish them. And KPIs were his barometer to see how his efforts were progressing.

In Jim's industry paychecks come bi-weekly so a KPI became how much of that paycheck he was able to use towards paying off debt. He started with a quarterly KPI of 20% per paycheck. Surprisingly, the more he kept tabs on this number, the more he wanted to increase this and began looking for ways to decrease his expenses. It became kind of a fun game. In quarter 3 of that first year, he went up to 30%, then he was close to 50% for the final year.

Something simple like tracking a percentage of a paycheck can help you stay on task towards your OKRs and SMART goal. Jim achieved his goal but more importantly he began to leverage KPIs in other areas to keep a pulse on the goals he set for himself and increase his chances of reaching them.

Exercises

1. Refer to your inner purpose you previously wrote and revise it if necessary
2. Create OKRs for the next 3 months.
3. Create KPIs related to those OKRs.

References

Schult, M. (2021) *The Exponential Entrepreneur*. Schult Publishing.

Chapter 9

Developing and Maintaining Habits

"Really, what matters in the long run is sticking with things and working daily to get better at them."
– Angela Duckworth

<u>Contributors</u>: Paola Hurtado, Eric Patel, Howard Rankin

Just do it.

Nike said it best…without action life remains at a standstill. Very few things will materialize in your life without you taking action to make things happen. Of course, like we discussed, the universe will do its thing; in the meantime, there is much you can manifest on your own. The brain will do its thing too. And as mentioned earlier your brain is incredibly elastic and can adapt amazingly if you think differently. Action is the key to change.

This part of the playbook provides you with the fuel to keep going which may be the hardest part of all of this: maintaining your momentum, progressing and not quitting.

Psychologists James Prochaska and Carlo DiClemente devised a five-stage model of change back in the 1980s. It is universal and is a very simple way to understand the formation of habits.

The five stages are:

- Precontemplation: Not even considering change.
- Contemplation: Thinking about it but not yet acting on it.
- Preparation: Getting organized to make change.
- Action: Implementing change.
- Maintenance: Continuing to maintain 'new' behaviors.

We don't want to just create a new habit; we want to make a habit that is resistant to change. And there's the challenge for many people. Most New Year's resolutions are abandoned within the first month after they're made. Going on a healthier, lower calorie diet for a couple of weeks is not a new habit. It's a start but it's not yet ingrained as a habit. A behavior is a habit when it's easily reinstated.

A habit develops when you have repeated the same behavior many times. Your brain changes and creates new neural pathways that underpin the new behavior. The more you repeat the behavior, the stronger those neural pathways become. And after more time, the neural imprint for those behaviors gets sent to a different part of the brain, the basal ganglia, which henceforth executes them without the need to consciously think about what to do.

The keys to creating a habit are:

- Always keep in mind the bigger purpose of the habit. For example, "I'm investing in myself and my health so I can perform at my peak potential."
- Make the behavior easier to achieve. You might say "I'm going to run at least two miles every day," rather than "I'm going to run five miles every day." You can always adjust your goal.

- Make it as enjoyable as possible. While you're out walking or running you can listen to music or an audiobook.
- Associate new habits with already existing ones, so they have anchors. For example, as you pick up your car keys you stop and think about what the keys to today's behavior change program are.

This doesn't mean that you become compulsive to complete your new routines every day. That might work in the short-term, but it is not practical over the length of time required to actually create a habit. Part of the problem with this approach is that it is based on the notion that if you miss a day then you're done. You have to be more flexible than that because with that extremely perfectionist mindset, if you miss a day, you might very well give up. It can be a self-fulfilling prophecy.

Life is about adaptation and so is habit change. You might have planned for a five mile walk today but the weather didn't cooperate, and other seemingly more important stuff needed attention. Now it's 7pm and you have barely walked 4000 steps (about two miles for the average person) all day. What are you going to do? You could go out for a 40-minute walk and probably double your daily steps to 8000. You could alter the rest of the week's schedule to compensate for the lost mileage. You could accept it was a tough day and not let it deflect you and continue with your planned schedule.

What you shouldn't do is take the day as proof that you can't do this and give up. Yet that is precisely what many people do. Moreover, some people quit just as they are about to make a breakthrough which raises a key issue about change.

Typically change doesn't occur dramatically. It occurs over time step-by-step. For example, you want to quit smoking. For six days you successfully avoid tobacco but on the seventh day you slip and have several cigarettes.

Now you could say to yourself, "I screwed up, I'm back to square one!" That's neither helpful nor true. The fact is that you have abstained from tobacco for six of the last seven days. If you don't use the thinking error to justify further smoking, you can keep going towards your goal. In the first month, you might have succeeded in not smoking for 26 of 30 days. If you don't self-sabotage and keep going, the next month you might abstain for 28 of 30 days. By the fourth month you might not have smoked at all.

This is why it is important to stay connected to your inner purpose. You need to stick to your ultimate goal and more importantly the reasons why that purpose is so important to you, keeping it in the forefront of your mind as much as possible. Develop your mantra and keep it visible around your environment. Think about it before going to bed. Visualize yourself executing actions that underpin that purpose.

This is where a coach, mentor, accountability buddy or support system can help. You can tell them what happened and why, get feedback that it's ok and your support person can follow up with you to ensure you adhere to your plan.

Maintenance is key to habit change. It's not just about doing something differently or new, it is about doing that new behavior long enough so that it becomes resistant to change.

Forming a habit is your next step to keep going. Habits are simply routine actions that you practice on a frequent basis.

Remember adaptation is critical. After you start, reflect on your experience and feelings you have about taking the action. If you do not like it, ask yourself why and adjust your plan accordingly.

To form a habit, you must define when and where you will repeat the action that you defined above. Techniques such as habit stacking help: define the habit as "I will do X after Y" where Y is something you already do routinely. For example, after I have my morning coffee I will sit down and write for 30 minutes. Track your progress day-to-day. How often do you want to engage in the habit and see how regularly you succeed? Reflect on your actions in relation to your inner purpose.

The real key is to not give up if you miss a day or fail to get started. This is an experiment! Learn from it. Build, measure and learn. Don't treat it as a chore but something you enjoy doing. If you don't enjoy doing it after a while, try something else.

Ask yourself: What's the problem/challenge you are currently facing? Is it aligned with my purpose? Is it important or impactful to solve this problem? Which area do you want to develop?

Define your action plan: list out things you need to do to make the goal become reality such as:

- I want to be a healthy person. In what ways can you be healthier?

- I would like to sleep more, eat healthier and exercise. What actions can you take today to get started?

Learn from experience on how to improve the chances of doing the new behaviors regularly enough over a long period of time to develop a change-resistant habit.

Now that you have assessed where you are, what resources you have, built a plan and started taking action, the attention must move to the "keep going" attitude. It's now time to go outside of yourself and leverage the relationships around you and create an accountability plan. Just as important as your action plan is, the internal governance you must have with yourself to make sure the momentum is kept and you achieve more than you expect is critical. Look for like-minded people, communities or groups where you can externalize your thoughts, learnings and insights and then check in with others.

Self-care

While self-care should already be a vital part of your practices it is mandatory to keep it going; minimizing stress, worry, anxiety and not getting burned out, should be a priority. Taking care of yourself and not ignoring or disregarding symptoms which can turn into problems is vital. Equally important is relaxation, rest, physical activity and of course, sleep.

The core attributes of a healthy and healing lifestyle are generally regarded as:

- Nutrition: A plant-based diet with minimal intake of processed foods, meat, dairy, sugar and alcohol.

- Physical Exercise: Approximately 150 minutes of aerobic activity a week. Some resistance exercises, ideally two or three times a week to keep muscles toned, and movement. Walking is a great activity and can easily be incorporated into a daily schedule. Getting at least 7,000 steps a day is a good target. The key is to have very few, if any, days of minimal activity, like 3000 steps.

- Sleep: Sleep is critical not just to restore energy and file away memories but also to clear the brain of toxins. 7-8 hours is the recommended amount for healthy sleep.

- Stress Management: We all experience stress but chronic stress is a serious health issue leading to inflammation and numerous potentially deadly diseases. Tools for effective stress management include activities like meditation, mindfulness, yoga, Tai chi and physical exercise.

- Cognitive and Social Stimulation: Social stimulation not only keeps us connected with others but helps develop and preserve empathy and compassion. Cognitive stimulation allows us to learn and develop and keep our cognitive functioning healthy.

- Healing: healing starts by acknowledging your limiting beliefs, your physical abilities and limitations and awareness of behavior that is triggered by primal states. Healing is then a decision: a decision that you are perfectly placed to solve a problem and/or contribute energetically to social impact.

- Celebration: it's also important that we remember to enjoy our progress, successes and wins. Celebrating is not something that should be left to special occasions. When warranted, even a little celebration goes a long way. And every small success is a special occasion.

The one thing that will move the needle the most to keep going especially when things get tough (and they will) is habitualizing things. Creating and sustaining habits helps minimize not only manual actions but repeated thought that could be better spent elsewhere.

Small Changes Can Make A Big Difference

Have you heard how small improvements can yield big results? Positive changes in life are interrelated. For example, suppose you make some small changes to your sleep routine that improve your overall length and quality of sleep. This is likely to have a trickle-down effect on your energy levels, physical activity, nutrition, attention and more.

Support and Inspiration

Asking for and leveraging help from others is something that many people are not accustomed to (let alone have a lot of experience or success with). Who says you have to go about this alone? You don't! And quite frankly, you shouldn't: not only do you increase your chance of success when you're being helped but it's more enjoyable and fulfilling along the way.

If at any point during the journey to develop an ExI mindset is most important, it's here. The mindset you formed and developed earlier in your journey, if properly fed and maintained, will carry you throughout your ups and downs.

Not quitting or making excuses is the name of the game. Solving problems, learning and moving on is critical. Once you decide to throw in the towel or give up it may be very difficult to get back on track and pick up where you left off. By being persistent and consistent you avoid this pitfall that so many have fallen into.

Sustaining change is difficult when done in a personal vacuum. You need others to help escape the tyranny of old habits and habitual thoughts. You need accountability so you can't just decide to abandon the journey. You need inspiration from others who have succeeded on similar journeys. You need the tools and advice that others who have walked the walk can give. You need other perspectives that can manage any exaggerated concerns that come from listening to your own thoughts. An effective group is a powerful tool for individual change and it is extremely valuable in your progress towards becoming an Exponential Individual.

Managing change

It is important to introduce the concept of flexible structure: that is, being disciplined enough to give yourself boundaries but flexible enough to change when external or internal stimulus requires it.

You shouldn't expect to control chaos but you can manage it by developing a system to process new information and for triaging. In the always-on, always-connected, instantaneous world we currently live in, everything that comes in "appears" urgent and important by its very nature that it found its way to us so fast. Managing change effectively means triaging and assessing through the lenses of urgency, importance and impact (big or small).

Personal Dashboard

Any effective tool to help us manage this process will be welcomed. Making all the elements of your life visible in the form of a dashboard not only keeps your progress in the forefront of your mind but also allows you to make on-the-fly course corrections instead of waiting to make a change when it is too late.

Find your personal effectiveness equilibrium: the balance between organization, structure, and well-being with these ideas:

- Get good at recognizing when you fall out of equilibrium.
- How do you manage change.
- Stop, start, continue.
- Changes make you revisit goals which in turn forces you to reevaluate actions.
- Can we create an image to reflect this relationship?

Regression To Previous Behaviors

The tendency and in some cases inevitability to return to a prior (inferior) state is always there. You must sustain your gains.

Significant fluctuations or regression to a prior state can cause doubt and despair.

Overestimate/Underestimate Problem

We tend to overestimate:

- How much time we have available for focused work.
- How many different things we can do at once.
- How much time we will have available in the future.

We tend to underestimate:

- How much time existing commitments will take (work and non-work).
- How many different things we have to do.
- How much time will be taken by unexpected commitments.

Embrace change by keeping these guidelines in mind:

- Expect to be disrupted.
- Prepare to be disrupted.
- Improve how you adapt.

One way to track progress is to go through the exercise of understanding one's motivators and drivers, identifying what is non-negotiable by way of values, ethics and wellbeing (self-care) and creating a map of the desired path. Then with whatever cadence makes sense (e.g. daily, weekly, monthly) evaluate alignment with those aspirations.

Exercises

1. Create a Vision Board: using either a paper-based or electronic method, post sayings, images and depictions of what your future state will look like
2. Track and asses your OKRs: periodically assess your progress against your OKRs and grade them

References

Anders Ericsson and Robert Poole. (2016) *Peak: Secrets of the New Science of Expertise.* Harper One.

Bill Burnett and Dave Evans. (2016) *Design Your Life: How to Build a Well-Lived Joyful Life.* Knopf

Brendon Burchard. (2017) *High Performance Habits: How Extraordinary People Become That Way.* Hay House
Clear, James. (2018) *Atomic Habits: An Easy & Proven Way to Build Good Habits & Break Bad Ones.* Avery

George Kohlrieser, Susan Goldsworthy et al. (2012) *Care to Dare.; Unleashing Astonishing Potential Through Secure Base Leadership.* Jossey-Bass

Michele Nevarez. (2021) *Beyond Emotional Intelligence: A Guide to Assessing Your Full Potential.* Wiley.

Olli Sovijarvi (2022) *Biohackers Handbook: Upgrade Yourself and Unleash Your Inner Potential.*

Prochaska, J. O., & DiClemente, C. C. (1983). Stages and processes of self-change of smoking: toward an integrative model of change. *Journal of consulting and clinical psychology, 51*(3), 390.

Simon Sinek. (2019) *The Infinite Game.* Portfolio

Links

How to Grade Your OKRs
https://www.whatmatters.com/faqs/how-to-grade-okrs

Chapter 10

Adjustment and Re-evaluation

"Adaptation seems to be, to a substantial extent, a process of reallocating your attention."
– Daniel Kahneman

Contributors: Karina Besprosvan, Steven Rodriguez, Dolapo Tukuru

You have now learned about tools that translate goals and dreams into actionable steps. You have learned how to identify your purpose and visualized an empowered life. You have even set OKRs and KPIs but perhaps things aren't going well. This next section is for you when:

- You are happy with where you are but want to do more for a better future.
- You are stuck where you are and want to figure out what to do to move forward.
- You are at a major transitional stage in your life or ready to start a new chapter in your life.
- You have a sense of urgency and want to transition from serving a small group of individuals to serving a group/team of individuals.

Here are some of the questions you asked and tried to answer in the previous parts of the playbook are:

- Who is an exponential individual?
- What is my purpose, truths and beliefs?
- Where am I at?
- Who do I want to become?
- How am I going to get there?

This section is about restarting but many of the tools also apply to getting started in the first place.

It looks as if you are already on your way. Somehow, you get stuck or lost in the moment or you want to do better and achieve more. You wonder if you should change direction or choose a different path to get to where you want to go. Where do you start?

Our suggestion is that you start where you are and take a new step forward. "How do I determine which step to take?" you might ask. "What is the next step?" This chapter is about helping you explore your options and take that new next step.

Here are some actions that will help you explore and determine your new next step:

1. Determine where you are.
2. You assessed where you are on the pillars of life and your position on the importance of helping others. You need to reevaluate where you are today.
3. You can also use The Wheel of Life to reassess where you are today. It currently lists the areas of life you can make an assessment both for your current state and your future state. You can modify the categories to be more relevant to your life situation. This simple tool can give you a sense of

which areas of life are more important to you than other areas and the gap between your current state (where you are today) and your future state (where you want to be). You can choose an area that's most important to you at the moment to start with.

4. Review your inner purpose using the following criteria:
   - Is it thrilling? Is it a source of inspiration for you? Is it what you care about? Is it what you want to do? Does it align with your personal values, interests, passions and sense of self?
   - Is it important? How much does it matter for you, your family, your community, your city, your country, your continent and globally?
   - Is it daunting? Does it make your palms sweaty and your stomach churn?

It is good to have a mix of the three elements. Thrilling gives you internal motivation, important gives you external motivation and daunting provides the engine of personal growth.

Review Where You Are

Determine where you are at the present. Based on where you want to go and what you want to become, assess the following:

- Where am I? Am I still working towards achieving my goals or am I drifting away from my goals?
- Am I on the right path? Do I need to change direction?
- Do I have the knowledge, time and courage to choose a new direction or take a new path?
- What are my pressing challenges and issues right now?

Determine the Next Step

Do you also feel the urgency of making some changes? Are you wondering "How do I really make it happen? What are my next steps?"

We suggest the following paths for you to explore:

- Based on what you learned about yourself, what has worked and what hasn't on your journey to becoming exponential?
  - If certain actions have produced the desired results, why?
  - If certain actions have failed, why?

- If you find it daunting to really figure out the first step yourself, you can always seek help from someone else: a mentor, a coach or someone who has more life experience than you and can give you guidance.

Review and Refresh

Some useful tips that apply to starting out on your journey or revising your plan include:

- Keep a journal: it could be digital or a paper journal. Write down how you feel and what comes to your mind when you are in your moment. Record any new insights you have.
- Take a systems approach: consider yourself part of a larger system. This system consists of many elements, each of

which can be further broken down to smaller elements. The system also has connections between elements. These elements and connections form patterns that help us make sense of the world around us. To better understand the world around us, it is useful to view yourself as part of the larger world and yourself, consisting of many elements connecting and interacting with each other.

- Keep a sketchbook. Use pen and paper to sketch out your thoughts. This virtual representation can provide a different viewpoint and perspective for you. The act of sketching is deeply meditative. It can reduce stress and increase happiness.
- Build out a situation, thought or an idea. By involving your hand in the thinking process this will also give you a different perspective.

Here are some additional tips that can help you get restarted:

1. Set your intention: revisit your goals and inner purpose. Ask yourself: What is my intention this week? What do I want to do, learn or achieve this week?
2. Use action verbs to describe what you will do to move yourself closer to where your intention is directing you.
3. Ask yourself: How will I know if I am closer to achieving my intention or not by the end of this week? How do I measure my progress?
4. Seek help: approach someone you deem to be successful, ask them how they got started

Live out loud. Build a community of people who can keep you accountable. Who can you report to? Who will keep you accountable and on track with your goals? Think about yourself as the steward and spokesperson of the desired outcomes (as opposed to owner). Your job is to recruit, delegate and not do everything.

Task-Oriented vs Action-Oriented

Tasks do not equal actions. We should be action oriented.

- Switch from being task-minded to action-minded.
- Task: a piece of work to be done or undertaken
- Action: the process of doing something, typically to achieve an outcome

	Tasks	**Actions**
Synonyms	Duty, Chore, Labor	Steps, Measures, Activity
How we measure success	Number of tasks completed	Progress against the outcome
Effective tools to manage	To-do list	Combination of Tools
Suited for	Highly Structured Work	Semi-structured and unstructured work

Action-Oriented vs Identity-Oriented

Start with goals and intention, turn nouns into verbs, e.g., reframe "I want to be a writer" to "I will write every day." For every goal you have, break it down into actionable items. For example,

- Intention: I want to lose weight.
- Type of person I want to become: I want to be a healthy person with energy and vitality.
- Action: I will eat healthy meals and run for 2 miles every day.

Keep a daily journal for tracking purposes. Be accountable to someone.

Experimentation

Once you decide on one goal you'd like to achieve you can start thinking about what actions you can take to move closer to achieve that goal. What can you do right now, this week, this month, this year, etc.? For things that are important but not immediately urgent, you need to develop a longer plan but with actions and a timeline to execute it.

Continuously learn and adjust: take action, measure, reflect, get feedback, learn, adjust, repeat.

It is also valuable to find actions that can impact multiple goals. For example, getting good sleep can improve your physical and mental health and can lead to a clearer mind, more energy and better mood which can lead to better relationships.

Start small: what can you do in 5 minutes, towards achieving a goal? Try to do it every day for a week. e.g., read 5 minutes, write for 10 minutes, etc.

It is important to prioritize and decide on what to tackle first. The Urgent vs Important matrix, also known as Eisenhower's Urgent/Important Principle, can be useful to set priorities:

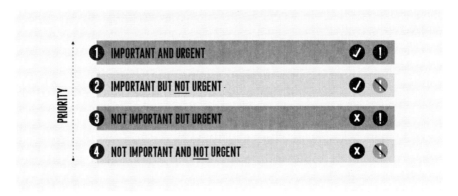

After you finish this part, you will be well on your way to restart your transformational journey to become an Exponential Individual.

Exercises

1. Prioritize your goals and make them actionable

List out your original goals. Have they changed and if so, how? What are your new goals? It may be helpful if you think about the areas of impact, e.g., social impact, financial impact, etc. This may help you align your goals with your life stages.

Order the goals in terms of personal importance and priority. Write down the top goal you have determined in the step above and answer the following questions:

- What actions can you take now, to get one step closer to achieve that goal?
- Now answer this question for each of the actions: Can you do this action by yourself or do you need help from someone else?

For the actions you can take now by yourself do the following:

Time / Impact (use a matrix to determine the efforts involved, i.e., time needed to take this action)

	Time / Effort low	Time / Effort high
Impact high	Action 1	Action 3
Impact low		Action 2

If the action seems too daunting to execute then you can break it down further into sub-steps. For example, if your action is to write a book, you can break it down into the following sub steps:

1. Schedule a block of time for writing every day.
2. Set up your workspace.
3. Create an outline.
4. Write 20-30 minutes daily.

Depending on your goals and prior knowledge your list will look different. You can modify and enhance this list as you gain more knowledge. You can also go deep down or stay at the higher level.

Starting is usually the hardest part. Commit to this exercise for a predetermined amount of time. You will find that once you start you may end up writing for longer than that and enjoy the process.

2. Transition from intention to action

1. Take out a piece of paper, write down 3 intentions you have for the next 7 days. For example, I want to be a better writer.

2. For each intention, think of 2 actions that you can do, using a verb to describe each. For example, I will write during each day.
3. For each action, think of a way to measure success. I will write for 10 minutes each day.
4. Write a summary sentence combining 1) your intention, 2) your action and 3) how you would track progress.

For example, to become a better writer, I will write each day for 10 min for the next 7 days.

References

Bungay Stanier, M. (2022). *How to Begin: Start Doing Something That Matters*. Page Two Books, Incorporated.

Burnett, W., Evans, D. J., & Burnett, B. (2016). *Designing Your Life: How to Build a Well-lived, Joyful Life*. Alfred A. Knopf.

Clear, J. *Atomic Habits: An Easy and Proven Way to Build Good Habits and Break Bad Ones.* Penguin Random House.

Fearne, M. (2020). *The LSP Method: How to Engage People and Spark Insights Using the LEGO(R) Serious Play(R) Method.* Lioncrest Publishing.

Nevarez, S. M. (2021). *Beyond Emotional Intelligence: A Guide to Accessing Your Full Potential.* Wiley.

Novogratz, J. (2020). *Manifesto for a Moral Revolution: Practices to Build a Better World.* Henry Holt and Company.

Wiseman, L. (2017). *Multipliers, Revised and Updated: How the Best Leaders Make Everyone Smarter.* HarperCollins.

Wiseman, L. (2021). *Impact Players: How to Take the Lead, Play Bigger, and Multiply Your Impact.* HarperCollins Publishers.

Links

Clear, J. (2018, August 7). *Atomic Habits: How to Get 1% Better Every Day* - James Clear. YouTube. Retrieved March 18, 2022, from https://youtu.be/U_nzqnXWvSo

Eisenhower Matrix:
https://www.mindtools.com/pages/article/newHTE_91.htm

How a sketchbook can change your life. (2021, May 15). YouTube. Retrieved March 18, 2022, from https://youtu.be/mWRki37iOzg

How to turn loss into inspiration | George Kohlrieser | TEDxLausanne. (2015, March 17). YouTube. Retrieved March 15, 2022, from https://youtu.be/RNwKV_Rk-TU

PDCA Cycle - What is the Plan-Do-Check-Act Cycle? (n.d.). ASQ. Retrieved March 18, 2022, from https://asq.org/quality-resources/pdca-cycle

10 Breathing Exercises to Try: For Stress, Training & Lung Capacity. (2019, April 9). Healthline. Retrieved March 18, 2022, from https://www.healthline.com/health/breathing-exercise

Think with your hands -- an introduction to the LEGO® SERIOUS PLAY® methodology. (2020, April 6). YouTube. Retrieved March 18, 2022, from https://youtu.be/APhJfZfpEyY

What is Meditation? Headspace. Retrieved March 18, 2022, from https://www.headspace.com/meditation-101/what-is-meditation

https://www.samuelthomasdavies.com/book-summaries/self-help/atomic-habits/

Wheel of Life: https://learningcollectives.github.io/wheeloflife/

Chapter 11

What's Next for the Greater Good?

"The only way that we can live is if we grow. The only way we can grow is if we change. The only way we can change is if we learn. The only way we can learn is if we are exposed. And the only way that we are exposed is if we throw ourselves into the open."
— C. Joybell

<u>Contributors</u>: Ann Boothello, Angela Faye, Julie Hamilton, Gerard Scheenstra

There is no right or wrong time to begin your personal transformation and self-awareness journey. Once you have made the choice to embark within, your "pandora's box" is open and it is difficult then to put the lid back on your curiosity.

Inevitably, opportunities are not always fairly distributed. It is becoming increasingly more important that we as a collective ensure that no one is left behind as much as we are able. Part of our own evolution to "pay it forward" may just be to influence those around us - even if it is just one person - for the better.

It is sometimes difficult to gauge what impact we have on others. Not everyone has access to mentors or role models, nor does everyone want to consciously self-discover. Life, however, has a way of teaching us what we need to learn to grow. Sometimes the people who trigger us or the ones we have left in our past may prove to be our biggest teachers; we just don't know it yet. In every moment we have a choice to learn or disregard what is showing up in our lives. Our hope is that we all choose to learn and through that, better ourselves moving forward.

Another point we'd like to raise is the impact that can come from the small gestures or actions we can take in the world whether that be praising someone for their achievements or casually making a negative remark. Both are important since the "good" and "bad" moments can shape us for the better. This depends on our self-awareness and ability to learn from life's lessons to fuel positive evolution of the self and thus the collective. Lessons can even be learned from people you least expect. The exchange of energy between people through conversations, actions or our unique gifts can be very powerful.

We are living in an era where our individual choices can significantly impact our collective evolution, for better or worse.

Leaving a better future for generations to come will require each one of us to discover, develop and contribute our unique gifts to alleviate the planetary challenges we face.

Self-awareness is a key component to preserving our planet and our humanity.

For our human interactions and interpersonal relationships to be more fulfilling, empathy, kindness and compassion are needed. This can be achieved if one is more self-aware. The result of this can cause a harmonious butterfly effect where one interaction influences another, and so on, to impact the collective positively. A positive interaction produces dopamine, the feel-good chemical produced in the brain, both in the recipient and the giver. A negative interaction however could leave a recipient in a stressful or angry mode. Stress triggers our brain to conclude that we are in danger, thus shifting us into survival (fight-or-flight) mode. This causes us to focus on the threat in front of us and ignore everything else, from the ability to find creative solutions to a problem to the body's ability to rest and repair itself. This means we are more susceptible to poor decision making and disease as our immunity drops in a state of chronic stress.

The more we collectively focus on a deeper level of self-awareness and cultivating lasting relationships, the more likely we are to achieve solutions for us all.

What potential pitfalls could be encountered if self-exploration and our relationship with others are not taken into consideration? What if we go out into the world without our own authentic personalized road map attempting to help everyone else?

For optimal results it's good to understand why, how, what, when and with whom you are considering co-creating with. Understanding yourself first, what makes you unique and then understanding others and their motivations are a good start. This kind of thinking is helpful and sustainable plus a daily check to see whether you are aligned to your purpose will guide you in your decision making. It is more than likely that by following these basic habits, your energy expended will be targeted and impactful. In other words, getting your own needs met is the first step along the path. You will then be more useful to others when collaborating with them. Without practicing this way of being, similar to being in an aircraft, if your own oxygen mask is not put on first then it is difficult to be there for others.

On the other hand, understanding oneself without intending to understand others dismisses the fact that we live within a collective and the way we choose to be and act has an impact on others.

What does the term "greater good" actually mean? What are the overriding benefits of this way of thinking?

Understanding our own personal needs and boundaries is important so we don't burn out. Serving the greater good starts with the understanding of how to serve ourselves.

Burn out was one of the primary causes of the Great Resignation and followed by Quiet Quitting highlighted by the COVID-19 pandemic. Burn out symptoms may include:

- Exhaustion
- Cynicism
- Depression
- Negativity
- Irritated
- Feeling useless
- Hating your job

One of the many accelerated pathways towards self-actualization is to focus on your individual inner purpose mentioned earlier. Once this is in place your personal energy can be optimized.

Once your individual inner purpose has been established and aligned towards a common purpose, ambition or goal, acceleration can be then achieved: collective greater good, transcendence or group flow is reached. This is where the magic happens: creativity, innovation and problem solving are increased and greater results can then be achieved by individuals for grand challenges for the greater good.

When you start to notice a higher-than-normal attraction occurring (e.g. people are approaching you rather you having to chase them), coincidences and serendipity happening, things are effortless and/or your performance is augmented, this is when you can be confident that your self-awareness, self-actualization and your outwards focus can really take off.

"Meeting people where they are at" relates to our ExI Principles (refer to the appendix or our website to see all of them). In other words, start wherever you find yourself and others and then go from there which means greater good projects can commence whether you are at the beginning, middle or end of your life journey. It's never too late to get started.

Case study

George was a successful businessman and retired into a very comfortable life. He looked forward to playing golf regularly and relaxing from the porch of his beachfront property. After six months of this luxurious lifestyle, George felt he was losing some of his cognitive abilities. Life wasn't as much fun as he thought it would be. In fact, there were days where he was downright depressed.

After seeking help from a professional, George realized that retirement for him should not be all play. He still needed a challenge; he still needed to exercise his considerable skills, he still needed a purpose greater than improving his golf handicap.

George started a local non-profit to help family caregivers, a major issue in his area where there were many aging parents needing daily care and supervision. George's energy and cognitive functions returned to their usual high levels. He had found his purpose for this stage of his life.

The state of the world at this moment in time is that we are a consumer-driven society (Homo Economicus) while we need to move to a We Driven society, designated as Homo Amans by Humberto Maturana.

In 1943 Abraham Maslow introduced the concept of a hierarchy of human needs. He originally had self-actualization as the top of the hierarchy but added another level of self-transcendence later in life. This upper level is not always reflected in Maslow's hierarchy. In a 1971 paper Maslow stated:

"Transcendence refers to the very highest and most inclusive or holistic levels of human consciousness, behaving and relating, as ends rather than means, to oneself, to significant others, to human beings in general, to other species, to nature, and to the cosmos."

Maslow argued that to have a great synergy within oneself is the highest level of motivation, of consciousness, of being in the world. When there is no separation between self and the world, what's good for you, is good for the world; that's synergy.

Dr. Clare Graves was a Professor at Union College, Schenectady, NY USA and a contemporary of Abraham Maslow. One of the biggest distinctions between Graves' work and that of Maslow was that the latter believed that there was a limit to human development (the levels of self-actualization) whereas Graves was convinced that there was no end. Towards the end of his life, Maslow acknowledged that he had been wrong in his conclusions.

Below is Maslow's model:

Graves further work extended to how individuals and communities are orientated and why past and current communities and individuals evolve and function.

The point where we find ourselves now in our evolutionary path comes from the materialistic (individual) to a personalistic (communal). This means after consuming huge amounts of silo "Me"-orientated items and achievements which only served us personally but at significant costs to the planet and our own species, we are now beginning to orient ourselves to a "We" way of being.

Going back to Maslow's theory, he explored what a synergistic society would look like; what would it mean for us to have self-actualizing societies (greater good ways of being) where virtue pays.

He recognized this would mean changing our whole reward structure. He had a term for this which he called "meta pay" and argued that transcenders, who are not motivated by money, could give money to all those who need it. We don't need to pay the transcenders as much, he said, their virtue will pay. Therefore, he argued, there should be no separation between what's good for you and good for the world.

This level both Maslow and Graves identified has perhaps never been more needed in humanity. It is one of the key components to our survival as a species and encompasses every aspect of our life on the planet.

We are now in charge of the choices we make and have made. Some choices we are still in control of. Others we have / had, could be slipping away or have slipped away if we as a collective don't wake up to the fact that we are in a significant evolutionary stage.

How we move forward is up to us and how we prioritize the things that are important and time sensitive, not just for ourselves but for the greater good, is now.

Metrics including how we measure, what we measure, how we reward ourselves and each other have kept the status quo for the few are slowly changing yet not quickly enough.

The problem has been us, operating as humans, in silos. The solution is us, operating as humans, collectively and collaboratively.

We are by no means there yet but an ecosystem is beginning to build and develop, so we are on the way.

The introduction of Web3, Decentralized Autonomous Organizations (DAOs), blockchain, tokenized systems and economies, could eventually and potentially be a complete redistribution of wealth. Tokenization could enable more greater good projects, cultures and communities. This was the original and often misunderstood intention and one of the reasons why Bitcoin was created: to disrupt the current banking and financial systems. As with any early edge concept, there have been some challenges along the way but the technological breakthroughs especially solving the unpopular energy consumption issues are gathering pace since Bitcoin launched.

Recall the Web2 era for a moment: the democratization (access to all, e.g., the internet) and demonetization (nominal or no fees for tools e.g. EventBrite) that have come from some of the most promising technological shifts of the last couple of decades brought about opportunities for all who have an internet connection to have baseline tools available.

Now with a quickening adoption of the Web3 movement, also known as the 'internet of value', the way we interact will shift from individualism, consumerism and information exchange to value exchange, cooperative ownership models and community building.

We are at the point in time where, as more individuals experience their exponentiality with or without knowing it, the influence of the collective will expand as people witness what is possible for others and what is possible for themselves. The evolution is not just of humanity but the planet, nature, animals and each and every aspect of life to form a whole. That is our most hopeful, exciting and potentially exponential reality where the integration of technology and highest levels of collective consciousness can converge.

To reach our collective greater good however starts from within, through ourselves as individuals. The term "show don't tell" is a good place to influence others so it is suggested that this is where we start. Once we have our own self-awareness or are curious about our own self-awareness, this is the first step on the journey to doing more for the greater good.

The good news is that it is already happening with leading frameworks and communities such as Exponential Individuals.

Here are some ways in which you can contribute to the collective:

- Listening: be a friend who lends an ear.
- Formal or informal mentorship in the form of story-sharing.
- Words and actions of encouragement and inspiration.

- Financial investment in people and communities.
- Coaching and reciprocal learning opportunities.
- Inviting and engaging others in your networks.

It is the recognition of the journey before - our past - which allows us to recognize our uniqueness, something no one else on the planet can replicate. If fully understood and sacred only to you, this is what can make the biggest impact in the world, however small.

We all have seeds within us when we are born. Our environment can affect us although this can be temporary. Trauma can affect us but can also galvanize us into prioritizing what's important. Death is an amazing leveler to assist our choice-making.

Understanding your starting point, each other's starting point, finding your triggers for your own flow and what's right for you will allow not just you to create the best life for yourself but also for those around you and ultimately the greater good.

It's time for disruption. To know you really existed and benefited others while you are here - whatever your current personality or background - appreciating the basic human needs each one of us has to share is a good place to start.

Let's unpack and repack, creating the shape we want for ourselves and by doing this, we can influence this most critical and vital component and that is our collective duty for a system change.

What can stop this? Understanding there is a spectrum of personalities, behaviors, beliefs, values, which are a complete 180 degrees opposite to ourselves, is critical. We should set a quest, each and every one of us, to understand our polar opposites so we may live more in harmony with our neighbors. None of us are exactly the same: everyone is unique as to where we find ourselves and in particular where we fall on various personality ranges. However, it is this simultaneous deep understanding of others which we must also consider in parallel to everything else that is going on around us in our daily lives.

References

Maslow, A. H. (1943). A theory of human motivation. *Psychological Review, 50(4)*, 370-96.

Maslow, A. H. (1954). *Motivation and personality*. New York: Harper and Row.

Maslow, A. H. (1962). *Toward a psychology of being*. Princeton: D. Van Nostrand Company.

Maslow, A. H. (1970a). *Motivation and personality*. New York: Harper & Row.

Maslow, A. H. (1970b). *Religions, values, and peak experiences*. New York: Penguin. (Original work published 1966)

Maslow, A. H. (1987). *Motivation and personality (3rd ed.)*. Delhi, India: Pearson Education.

Graves, Clare W. (September–October 1966). "Deterioration of Work Standards". Harvard Business Review. 44 (5): 117–126

Graves, Clare W. (October 22–24, 1969). A Systems View of Values Problems. Systems Science & Cybernetics Conference. IEEE No. 69-C37-SSC.

Graves, Clare W. (April 1974). "Human Nature Prepares for a Momentous Leap". The Futurist. pp. 72–87.

Graves, Clare W. (Fall 1970). "Levels of Existence: An Open System Theory of Values". Journal of Humanistic Psychology. 10 (2): 131–155. doi:10.1177/002216787001000205. S2CID 144532391.

Links

"Humberto Maturana, *Metadesign*, part III August 1, 1997". Archived from the original on May 11, 2015. Retrieved January 21, 2016.

tns.pdf (thenetworkstate.com)

Rebalancing Society | Henry Mintzberg
9781626563179.pdf (mintzberg.org)
(1) Henry Mintzberg on Rebalancing Society (Full Seminar) - YouTube

Donald Hoffman: Reality is an Illusion - How Evolution Hid the Truth | Lex Fridman Podcast #293 - YouTube

Brian Muraresku: The Secret History of Psychedelics | Lex Fridman Podcast #211 - YouTube

Co-Creation: A Powerful Tool For Organizations Looking To Become More Innovative (forbes.com)

To find work you love, don't follow your passion | Benjamin Todd | TEDxYouth@Tallinn - YouTube

Chapter 12

Dare to Live

<u>Contributors</u>: Howard Rankin

If you have gotten this far in the book you will have read about the different practices and tools that can help to make you an Exponential Individual. While these resources are great there's something more important than all of them: you.

Any one of us, no matter where we are at in life, can choose the next phase of our existence. If you are young and stuck, do you just want to stay stuck? You can be stuck forever but you won't be young forever. Life is about adaptation. It's about learning, mostly about yourself. And let's not forget that the brain isn't fully developed until at least the mid-twenties, if not later. Even if you are still unsure about your direction there's one thing you can commit to: being daring enough to live fully, develop skills and help your fellow human beings.

You might be in mid-life, coasting along in a somewhat rewarding career that offers financial stability. That's fine. But what can you do outside the workplace? Can you find meaningful activities that enhance you as a person while helping others? Perhaps you can use your love of a sport and related skills to coach a team or teach children how to play and enjoy a sport. Sometimes our most meaningful activities are those that inspire, teach and help others, without any financial gain by not serving as an employee or C-suite executive.

You might be a retiree who, like George from our earlier case study, thought that playing golf every day would be fun and relaxing. After all, he worked hard all his life to get to this point. However, after a few weeks of doing this something seemed missing. There was no sense of contribution or meaning. Then, like George, you also may come to realize that retirement isn't one long vacation. It's another chance to learn, exercise your skills and help others. You don't have to go back to work, you just have to put meaning back into your life: volunteer your immense knowledge, capacities and skills to enhance the lives of others. Don't just consider contributing financially to causes that are important to you, try to be more involved, make a difference and ultimately have an impact on leaving your legacy.

At every stage of life there are immense opportunities to offer our talents and skills to enhance life in general, not just for ourselves but for others. For most of us there's no better feeling or accomplishment than helping others so that they too, can take another step on their journey to living their best life.

When you dare to live you are also being a role model, an inspiration to others who see not just your successes but also your immense satisfaction and leveraging yourself for the well-being of others. Is there any better feeling?

Dare to Live!

Try looking at tomorrow not yesterday
And all the things you left behind
All those tender words you did not say
The gentle touch you couldn't find

In these days of nameless faces
There is no one truth but only pieces
My life is all I have to give

Dare to live until the very last
Dare to live forget about the past
Dare to live giving something of yourself to others
Even when it seems there's nothing more left to give

But if you saw a man
In front of your door
Sleeping wrapped in a cardboard,
If you listen to the world one morning
Without the noise of the rain,
You can create with your voice,
You, think of the people's thoughts,
Then God is just God.

To live, no one has ever taught us,
To live, you can not live without the past,
Living is beautiful even if you have never asked for it,
It will be a song, someone will sing it.

Dare to live searching for the ones you love,
(Why, why, why, why not live tonight?)
Dare to live no one but we all,
(Why, why, why, why not live now?)
Dare to live until the very last,
(Why, why, why is life not life?)
Your life is all you have to give (Because)
You did not live it
To live!

Dare to live until the very last,
(Why, why, why is life not life?)
Your life is all you have to give (Because)
You have never lived

I will say no (I will say yes)
Say dare to live
Dare to live

About ExI

Exponential Individuals (ExI) is comprised of a group of global leaders, published authors and human transformation enthusiasts focused on assisting people across the globe evolve their way of being into one that encourages individual authenticity, community collaboration and care, deep healing and a sense of interconnected responsibility to create a better future for all.

Our moonshot is to help over 1 billion individuals by 2040 harness the power that lies within themselves to live more fulfilled lives. We serve as a catalyst to make self-awareness, human optimization and collective betterment universal.

Playing at the intersection of exponential technologies and elevating consciousness, Exponential Individuals is set to become the leading global Web3 ecosystem for personalized human transformation solutions and community support.

Learn more at exponentialindividuals.io

ExI Principles

1. Freedom of Inner-Exploration

The ExI Initiative is a "no teach and no preach" zone. We encourage the exploration of an ever-evolving landscape of knowledge, from scientific research to ancient wisdom, to tools, techniques, technologies and belief systems that support transcending one's limited self into a being that is fully 'alive' and living aligned to purpose. We believe in preserving & honoring ancient wisdom to live well, healthy and long. We embrace developments in modern science and technology to catalyze the awareness needed to fully explore our inner world and drive impactful change in the world.

2. Purposeful Action

Purpose comes from a lifelong journey of deep self-awareness. ExI members believe in an ever-evolving life of purpose. In our everyday behavior, we stay open to exploration of the self through habituating stillness, reflection, gratitude and purposeful action. All interactions by members should reflect one's authenticity. There should be genuine care of the consequences of one's actions on mankind, animals and the environment.

3. Preservation of Nature

ExI members are conscious of the need for regeneration of our environment and are considerate in their use of resources. ExI members ensure that any solutions they create are mindful of preserving the climate and nature through their personal behavior and communal actions.

4. Mutual Respect & Appreciation For All paths

At ExI we treat each other with integrity in an open and respectful way. We expect all members to contribute to such culture while ExI ensures the conditions for this. Discrimination will not be tolerated. ExI promotes the protection of and compliance with human rights while acceptance of diverse values is essential.

Community events will always observe the concerns for public welfare and communicate civic responsibilities to participants in accordance with local laws. We further adhere to the principles of fair trade and competition supporting and respecting the intellectual property of our peers, our clients, our competitors and our business partners.

5. Active Listening

Test this hypothesis in every group discussion: "It's often the quietest ones in the room, with the most well-rounded thoughts, and boldest ideas." Often there are always the usual suspects who steal the spotlight, this is great as all are welcome to contribute and some are gifted with the art of story-telling; however, we need to remain mindful of allowing ways to exist where those who don't like the spotlight can share their views for consideration by the community. Even if he/she does not present them in front of the entire group, we need to ensure that there are ways by which these thoughts are allowed to be expressed.

6. Every Challenge Requires An Entrepreneurial Spirit That's Hungry For Solutions

When something is not ok, whether it is a relationship conflict, confusion as we live more in surrender or we hit a roadblock in life/work/love/energy, what does an ExI do? We energetically shift it. Some of us may voice it. Some of us may heal it in silence. However, we are of the mindset and heartset that if there is something off, there is something we can learn from it and something we can do to resolve it for the better. Hence, we live with a solutions mind-set and encourage anyone who feels strongly that something should be done differently to be the change, don't just want it. How? By offering one or more solutions to tackle the challenge, energetically manifest healing and guidance or by conveying an opinion in a respectful and constructive manner to influence the individual/team/community towards something better. We can also agree to disagree, in which case multiple ideas can be tested, or relationships can be mended by amicably coming to a mutually beneficial agreement on how to move forward.

7. Aligned Action & Accountability

ExI members are committed to delivering solutions to make "self awareness and human optimization universal," pivoting ideas when necessary while always staying true to ExI's principles and purpose. They are empowered, driven individuals who hold themselves accountable to their commitments within the initiative and are open and honest if they can not follow through.

8. Inclusion, Education and Expansion

ExI is committed to radically inclusive ethics. We believe that transformative change, whether for an individual or in a society, can occur only through the medium of deep personal involvement. Everyone is invited to work. Everyone is invited to develop in pursuit of a more evolved, emotionally intelligent and fairer society and work and life conditions for all parties involved, letting them participate in the process of the build-up and strengthening of the organization. Therefore, all parties with an interest in the development should be involved in the collaborative process that relies on mutual education and the active encouragement to expand the basis of ExI as a global collaborative ecosystem on individuals driven for the greater good.

9. Radical Transparency

Friendship is built on trust. To create trust, you need radical transparency. This means that ExIs act with honesty, empathy and compassion. They are authentic, straight-up, humble, independent and action-oriented thinkers. Radical transparency helps us live these principles more accurately. We do not use misleading information in regard to the ExI. It is understood that no act of dishonesty, corruption or similar course of action that might harm ExI's reputation is ever an option for an ExI member. Moreover, ExIs act in a politically-neutral manner and are not influenced by any external political or economic interest.

10. Assume The Best In Others But Be Discerning

When co-creating with a global community, it's easy to get overwhelmed, feel misunderstood, get lost in the noise and point fingers; assume the best in others regardless. Show kindness, empathy and practice courage when creating with others. However, be discerning when you sense you or another may be disrespected, taken advantage of or manipulated. In this case being discerning to make a well-rounded decision for the benefit of yourself and/or the community on how to go about the situation. Bad players do exist. Do not be naive. Seek kinship in another community member if you need an opinion on how to proceed. Be there for yourself and others in the community. And never fear asking for a helping hand.

11. Deep Embodiment

It's easy to paint a picture of what we ideally want to see in the world and how we expect others to behave but not so easy to show up in the world and treat others in that same manner. Self-improvement and awareness are key to live by the ExI ethos. Be that which you want to see in the world and inspire others through action to transform for the better.

12. The Best Of Both Worlds

The virtual world and the real world can co-exist beautifully if people create conscious solutions. With the metaverse becoming a predominant topic, the possibilities it presents are endless. What can we do to enable living more fully in the 'real world' while benefiting from the evolution into Web3 and beyond? We exercise an awareness of the anxiety caused by the attention economy and lack of embodied interpersonal skills and wish to create solutions that steer away from that. Our goal is to create conscious solutions for humanity's overall well-being, agency and potential using tech where best fitted as an amplifier for it.

13. Collective Betterment

Our reason for being is to be the home for the planetary shift of consciousness: to evolve for the betterment of our own lives and thus influence the collective positively. As more individuals are inspired to embody their unique gifts and begin to live more fulfilled lives, others too will seek the shift within. This in turn we believe will have a knock-on effect on the love, energy and time we offer to help our fellow 'brothers and sisters' out. We believe no one should be left behind. Hence creating a more equitable future to evolve the human spirit into one that can not only accept our individual differences but come together stronger anyway, because of it, to serve in our collective evolution.

Acting individually for the good of all is the central idea behind our actions.

Contributing Authors

Kevin Allen

Kevin Allen is an energetic and creative individual. He believes that we live in an abundant world and looks for ways to impact those around him with positivity, especially through exponential technologies and the Exponential Organizations (ExO) Model. Kevin is the Chief Community Officer at OpenExO, an organization that drives the ExO Model through a global community in over 130 countries, in order to transform the world for a better future. Kevin is also a passionate traveler having visited 29 countries, loves nature and the outdoors and enjoys a good philosophical debate.

Karina Besprosvan

Karina Besprosvan is a human behavior expert and specialist in Consumer Insight, engagement and community development; with extensive experience working in multicultural environments and Fortune 100 companies. She has written over 50 papers and studies and has served as a guest speaker at over 100 industry events worldwide. She is also a co-author and editor of a variety of publications, including her #GenZRuleZ popular research about Generation Z. Karina is a Singularity University alumnus, OpenExO certified coach and trainer. She has an MA in Consumer Behavior, and Business Planning for women minorities, with a BA in Sociology, a BA in Marketing and Advertising, and a bachelor with teacher orientation.

Ann Boothello

Ann Boothello is an impact-for-good entrepreneur, author, speaker, coach, poet, dancer and philanthropist. She focuses on building initiatives that serve in upgrading society's concept of wealth and well-being. She serves as co-founder of Exponential Individuals, co-director at Unit Ventures Web3 Accelerator and Chief Culture Officer at BostonExO, besides her other pursuits. She has 14+ years of experience holding senior leadership roles in the online marketplace arena, real estate industry and the advertising industry. She is a Singularity University, Flow Genome Project and MIT Sloan Artificial Intelligence and Business Strategy alumna. Her passion lies at the intersection of consciousness, art and technology. Ann believes that leaders who heal well, lead well - enabling them to better the level of fulfillment in their own lives and inevitably that of the collective.

Anthony Boschi

Anthony Boschi believes it's time to revive philosophy. His curiosity and creativity has led him to dive into abstract writing where the patterns, forms and blueprints of human nature can be uncovered and expressed. It is in this burning passion where Anthony has found himself as a TEDx Speaker, a designer of programs on Emotional Intelligence and the host of Philosophy Cafe, a podcast that can be found on his YouTube channel. His academic background entails a degree in Psychology and Neuroscience as well as certification in Technology Management and Entrepreneurship. He encourages everyone to ask themselves one of his favorite questions: "What could you build if you created more than you consumed?"

Marco ("Mac") Carvalho

A seasoned IT professional, married to his first girlfriend for 40 years now, dad of 3 kids, IT entrepreneur for 36 years, professional coach and mentor for 15 years, forever musician and spiritualist practitioner, builds his purpose path on top of step stones that contribute to a better world for technology learning. Marco studies electronics, telecommunications, business management, IT management, philosophy, coaching and mentoring. Marco has served as a volunteer as director and mentor on several non profit organizations, related to IT and social causes.

Philip Earnhart

Philip Earnhart is a Swiss-American contemporary painter, graphic designer and philanthropist. Inspired from a young age by the tragic death of his brother to cancer and an increasing awareness of and empathy with outsiders, he rebelled against his strict evangelical upbringing to develop an artistic technique purely focused on his drive to create connections with the oppressed, the misunderstood and the burdened. His paintings are both active and contemplative, and they resonate with both urgency and humor. A critical exploration of the dualities of darkness and light, grief and resilience, oppression and freedom; the energy he discovers within these tensions is released in vibrant bursts of color that inspire the viewer and echo with the potential for deeper resolution.

Niki Faldemalaei

Co-Founder, Board Advisor, new CEO Community Experience Officer, Ambassador to Web3 Utility, Communications Consultant, Founder Extended Health Span Index & ExO Angels, Governor Island. Flywheel projects in the works include: Predict My Health Platform, My Bodytune Biometric Monitoring

Companion, Open ExO Founders Community, SingularityU San Diego Chapter Leadership, Abundance 360 Digital Community, Health Nucleus Research Subject. While working with the Newspaper Association of America, IMG Creative and Proelite, Niki achieved successful client placements in USA Today, Newsweek, Washington Post, New York Times, Huffington Post, Muscle & Fitness; at the Cannes Film Festival and Toronto Film Festival; as well as on the Sundance Channel, National Geographic Channel, and Showtime. Niki has also earned agency, publishing and New York Times interactive awards.

Angela Faye
Angela's massively transformative purpose is *Imagining and Building Places Worth Living For*. With plans to live to 147 years old, she looks forward to several more decades helping develop desirable, viable live, work, play destinations. Her working geniuses are galvanizing - rallying and motivating people around projects, ideas or initiatives - and discernment - making sound judgements relying on instincts and intuition across a wide variety of situations through pattern recognition and integrative thinking. Her style is outgoing, calm and achievement-focus. Three entrepreneurial parents - a farmer, a travel agent and an educator - helped shape her optimist, autonomous, future-focused outlook on life, and her family keep her energized, motivated and connected to the magic of daily life.

David Forman
David is an entrepreneur and futurist who operates at the crossover between technology and art. He holds degrees in both physics and music composition, and has built a variety of different startups ranging from game development, crypto fintech, aerospace, and

personal transformation. His MTP is to help a billion people become more intentional about their lives by leveraging the ancient skills of mindfulness and reflection.

Danielle Alice Desanges Aucéane THIAM MÉKÀ de GOGUENHEIM

Founder of TMG-NATEXO.Orion, LLC, Danielle is an energetic, curious and forward-thinking leader who leverages cybersecurity and exponential technologies to turn every idea into a value proposition and new business models to solve real world problems by leading the development and execution of projects and products to spark innovation, drive value creation, development, improvement and business growth for companies, industries and stakeholders. Danielle is telecommunications engineer with a background in STEAM although today her education reaches well beyond that scope because she is always eager to learn and acquire new knowledge, hard work never bothers her she loves facing challenges.

Julie Hamilton

Julie is a UK based entrepreneur. She founded her first business in 1989 selling it 4 years later which is when her interest in human performance and personal development, became apparent. Having qualified in various psychological and business tools, around 1994 to 2005 her London based human resources consultancy and latterly in 1998 search & selection business served some of the highest profile businesses in the UK. Her contribution to the UK IT industry conversation included appearing on UK TV (BBC), featuring both in The Institute of Directors and Computing Magazine plus The Financial Times, main conference speaker at a number of Computing Magasine's careers conferences. Since 2013 building on from her earlier career in the personal development space, her practice continues to work with high profile C-suite professionals and entrepreneurs. Her other business interests are a Web3 climate change and a fairness project plus raising consciousness relating to humanity and the planet.

Paola Hurtado

Paola Hurtado is a change maker with a mantra: *impossible is temporary, impossible is nothing.* She is a doer with an exponential mindset. She believes in human potential to create a better world. Paola is passionate about technology, innovation and life sciences. She has a PhD in Biotechnology and Chemical Technology, with a Degree in Environmental Sciences and Masters in Spectroscopy and Chemical Physics. She is a Stanford LEAD alumna, a year program with a strong focus on business innovation and leadership skills, and she has several certifications in innovation frameworks, such as Exponential Organizations, Purpose Launchpad, Design Thinking and Lean Startup. Paola is the Head of Strategic Projects at Universal DX and also serves as Chief Strategy Officer at BostonExO.

Eric Patel

Eric Patel serves as co-founder at Exponential Individuals and Chief Innovation Officer at BostonExO. He's a 5x startup company founder and is helping the ExO Economy bring the EXOS token to market and OpenExO's Web3 Transform DAO to life. Eric thrives as an author, speaker, coach, mentor and philanthropist. He holds certifications in QA, project management, innovation, agile, scrum and ExO. Eric also serves as an ambassador for OpenExO, Purpose Alliance and Rutanio, a mentor with Queens College Tech Incubator and the University of Pecs and shared in a 2021 ExO Transformation Award.

Howard Rankin

Dr. Howard Rankin has extensive expertise and knowledge in the areas of psychology, neuroscience, and behavior change. Dr. Rankin has written 12 books in his own name, co-written another 12 and ghostwritten 30 others, all nonfiction. Howard has also published more than 30 scientific articles on addiction and behavior change, and been a consultant to the NIH and WHO as well as editor of a major psychological journal. Howard is also a Psychology Today blogger, the creator and host of the How Not To Think podcast and Science Director at predictive analytics company IntualityAI.

Steven A. Rodríguez

Steven A. Rodríguez is a Fractional Operations Specialist for Hire Runner, Founder & Board for SUEGO and partner for CrowdWork DC LCA. He previously championed startup programs across the US & Canada for Techstars and the Global Entrepreneurship Network, and is on the Advisory Board for the Tech Incubator at Queens College. Steven has been a Startup Advisor for the U.S. Department of State's Young Leaders of the Americas Initiative (YLAI) and the Entrepreneurship World Cup, and an implementing partner for nationally- and globally renowned initiatives like 1 Million Cups for the Ewing Marion Kauffman Foundation and ExO Economy for OpenExO. Steven is an award-winning Community Professional (CMX Awards), distinguished CEmprende Ambassador (iNNpulsa Colombia) and rising Disruptive Innovation Specialist (OpenExO).

Gerard Scheenstra

Gerard Scheenstra is a visionary business leader and community builder with a unique set of superpowers. As a natural dot connector, he excels at bringing together people, businesses and ideas to create thriving communities and successful business models. With his sixth sense, he is able to listen and feel between the lines, gaining insights others might miss. Gerard's key mission and inner purpose is to promote "WE" thinking and doing. He is passionate about collective engagement and unlocking the superpowers of people, teams and organizations to create fit-for-future readiness.

Mynor Schult

Mynor has been a driver of strategic corporate expansion with extensive management experience in the USA and Latin American markets. He has delivered millions of dollars in shareholder value in the Aviation, Telecom, and Tourism industries. Currently, he's advising boards of directors, leadership teams and bold entrepreneurs on value creation, innovation and strategies to develop exponential organizations. Mynor, using his vast experience in corporate America, assists entrepreneurs with start-up innovation and accelerating technologies. His main purpose is to raise the standard of living in Latin America by teaching entrepreneurs digital technologies to transform their businesses into exponential organizations.

Dolapo Tukuru

Dolapo Tukuru is a strategy consultant with over 18 years experience working with FMCG, automobile, retailing, manufacturing, oil and gas, finance and education sectors. He is the Principal Consultant of Eduxtra Solutions Ltd. and a founding member of Strategic Management Forum, UK. He is a visiting Business Strategy facilitator to leading business schools in Africa including the Lagos Business School where he has taught and consulted on strategy issues for over 12 years. As a Certified ExO Consultant he provides turnaround and disruptive business solutions to corporations in Nigeria and sub-Saharan Africa. His massive transformation Purpose is to democratize quality education across Africa.

If you have enjoyed this book, please feel free to recommend it to your friends and colleagues. If you're so inclined, we would welcome a review on the Amazon page here…

https://www.amazon.com/Exponential-Individual-Playbook-Transform-Spirit-ebook/dp/B0BZ13SG78/ref=sr_1_1?crid=1PQ3ELNXQE2I7&keywords=exponential+individuals&qid=1681569607&s=books&sprefix=exponential+individuals%2Cstripbooks%2C100&sr=1-1

Thank you!!